What readers are saying about Michelle Robinette's Macs For Teachers...

"Teachers do battle all day long — against limited resources, crowded class-rooms, and demanding school boards. They don't need additional frustration from the computer. Michelle Robinette is heaven-sent: who else but an all-in-one teacher, writer, and Mac goddess could pull off a book this important as well?" — David Pogue, Contributing Editor, Macworld and author of IDG Books bestselling *Macs For Dummies,* 3rd Edition

"Just a quick note to let you know that your book made more sense and helped me more than any classes I've taken." — Diane Pease, Fourth Grade Teacher, Madison Public Schools, Madison, WI

"Teachers have needed a book like this for years! This fun, informative read is long overdue." — Gracie Pauly, ORBIS Software

"This is a thank you for lots of hard work for the FIRST ever real Mac book for teachers. I just spent my evening under the covers reading cover to cover! Great great great." — Kathleen Ferenz, San Francisco State University Instructor, and Eighth Grade Social Studies Teacher, Ben Franklin Middle School, Daly City, CA

"I love Michelle's writing style, experience, and examples." — Dr. David Henderson, Sam Houston State University, Department of Curriculum and Supervision

"I really like how you cut through the clutter to give helpful hints and info. Your book has already given me confidence and answered lots of my 'what on earth is this for?' questions." — Beverly Turner, First Grade Teacher, Rowlett, TX

"I am absolutely thrilled that teachers finally have a 'technological resource' developed especially for them." — Sandra J. Zapino, Technology Coordinator, Kenwood Elementary, Miami, FL

"I think it is great! This is exactly the type of hands-on information that teachers need." — Richard J. O'Conner, Ed.D., University of Arkansas, School of Education

"I have read (twice) your book *Macs For Teachers* and love it. Keep writing and keep teaching." — Vera McPike, Second Grade Teacher, Platte County District, Kansas City, MO

"I just finished your book and I thought it was a great reference for teachers. I thought all your software recommendations were right on target. Thanks for a great read and a great reference for teachers." — Lynne La France, Learning Support Teachers, Tunkhannock Area Middle School, Tunkhannock, PA and Adjunct Professor of Education at College Misericordia, Dallas, PA

"Michelle hasn't forgotten what it is like to be a teacher. This book has shown me that a computer can be used for more than educational games." — Sue Delaney, Chicago

"Finally! A quick glance reference book for *real* teachers." — Shannon McMillen, LaGrange, GA

"Thanks, Michelle, for easing the pain of using the Mac with children!" — Joan Burger, Fairbanks, AK

References for the Rest of Us!®

COMPUTER BOOK SERIES FROM IDG

Are you intimidated and confused by computers? Do you find that traditional manuals are overloaded with technical details you'll never use? Do your friends and family always call you to fix simple problems on their PCs? Then the ... *For Dummies®* computer book series from IDG Books Worldwide is for you.

... *For Dummies* books are written for those frustrated computer users who know they aren't really dumb but find that PC hardware, software, and indeed the unique vocabulary of computing make them feel helpless. ... *For Dummies* books use a lighthearted approach, a down-to-earth style, and even cartoons and humorous icons to diffuse computer novices' fears and build their confidence. Lighthearted but not lightweight, these books are a perfect survival guide for anyone forced to use a computer.

Already, hundreds of thousands of satisfied readers agree. They have made ... *For Dummies* books the #1 introductory level computer book series and have written asking for more. So, if you're looking for the most fun and easy way to learn about computers, look to ... *For Dummies* books to give you a helping hand.

IDG
BOOKS
WORLDWIDE

MAC® MULTIMEDIA FOR TEACHERS™

MAC®
MULTIMEDIA
FOR
TEACHERS™

by Michelle Robinette

Foreword by Steve Wozniak

IDG Books Worldwide, Inc.
An International Data Group Company

Foster City, CA ♦ Chicago, IL♦ Indianapolis, IN ♦ Braintree, MA ♦ Dallas, TX

Mac® Multimedia For Teachers™

Published by
IDG Books Worldwide, Inc.
An International Data Group Company
919 E. Hillsdale Blvd.
Suite 400
Foster City, CA 94404

Library of Congress Catalog Card No.: 95-79930

ISBN: 1-56884-603-7

Printed in the United States of America

10 9 8 7 6 5 4 3 2

1A/RR/RQ/ZV

Distributed in the United States by IDG Books Worldwide, Inc.

Distributed by Macmillan Canada for Canada; by Computer and Technical Books for the Caribbean Basin; by Contemporanea de Ediciones for Venezuela; by Distribuidora Cuspide for Argentina; by CITEC for Brazil; by Ediciones ZETA S.C.R. Ltda. for Peru; by Editorial Limusa SA for Mexico; by Transworld Publishers Limited in the United Kingdom and Europe; by Al-Maiman Publishers & Distributors for Saudi Arabia; by Simron Pty. Ltd. for South Africa; by IDG Communications (HK) Ltd. for Hong Kong; by Toppan Company Ltd. for Japan; by Addison Wesley Publishing Company for Korea; by Longman Singapore Publishers Ltd. for Singapore, Malaysia, Thailand, and Indonesia; by Unalis Corporation for Taiwan; by WS Computer Publishing Company, Inc. for the Philippines; by WoodsLane Pty. Ltd. for Australia; by WoodsLane Enterprises Ltd. for New Zealand.

For general information on IDG Books Worldwide's books in the U.S., please call our Consumer Customer Service department at 800-762-2974. For reseller information, including discounts and premium sales, please call our Reseller Customer Service department at 800-434-3422.

For information on where to purchase IDG Books Worldwide's books outside the U.S., contact IDG Books Worldwide at 415-655-3021 or fax 415-655-3295.

For information on translations, contact Marc Jeffrey Mikulich, Director, Foreign & Subsidiary Rights, at IDG Books Worldwide, 415-655-3018 or fax 415-655-3295.

For sales inquiries and special prices for bulk quantities, write to the address above or call IDG Books Worldwide at 415-655-3200.

For information on using IDG Books Worldwide's books in the classroom, or ordering examination copies, contact Jim Kelly at 800-434-2086.

For authorization to photocopy items for corporate, personal, or educational use, please contact Copyright Clearance Center, 222 Rosewood Drive, Danvers, MA 01923, or fax 508-750-4470.

 is a trademark under the exclusive license to IDG Books Worldwide, Inc., from International Data Group, Inc.

About the Author

Michelle Robinette is a self-taught specialist in the area of educational computing. She developed an interest in computers during her first year as an elementary school teacher when an Apple IIe was placed in her classroom. There were no instructions to follow — just a computer. She taught herself how to use it and was soon considered to be the local expert in conducting inservices and workshops showing others how easily technology could be integrated into the everyday curriculum.

Eight years later, Michelle now serves as the technology coordinator for a large elementary school in metro Atlanta. She enjoys helping teachers overcome their "technophobia" and is on a quest to merge technology and curriculum in an effort to make technology a natural part of the education process — not a subject within itself.

Michelle and her husband, John, live in the suburbs of Atlanta. Their days (and nights) are kept busy caring for their four-year-old daughter Jessie (who wants to be a princess when she grows up), their two-year-old son John-Michael (who calls all dogs *foo-foos* and cries when it's time to come inside), Sarah and Toby (their lovable golden retrievers), and Chelsea (an old gray cat).

In an earlier life (her early twenties), Michelle earned a degree in journalism from Georgia State University (which, to her parents dismay, she never used — until now) and spent a couple of wild and crazy years as an NFL cheerleader for the Atlanta Falcons. She later earned her teaching credentials from the University of Georgia and went on to receive her Master's and Specialist degrees in education.

Michelle's other goals and aspirations include coauthoring a children's story with her daughter Jessie, becoming a professional storyteller, and writing screenplays for wholesome family movies.

If Michelle could have it her way, every parent would spend a day as a teacher in order to appreciate fully the demands of the job — a rainy day without a recess break.

Welcome to the world of IDG Books Worldwide.

IDG Books Worldwide, Inc., is a subsidiary of International Data Group, the world's largest publisher of computer-related information and the leading global provider of information services on information technology. IDG was founded more than 25 years ago and now employs more than 7,500 people worldwide. IDG publishes more than 235 computer publications in 67 countries (see listing below). More than 70 million people read one or more IDG publications each month.

Launched in 1990, IDG Books Worldwide is today the #1 publisher of best-selling computer books in the United States. We are proud to have received 8 awards from the Computer Press Association in recognition of editorial excellence, and our best-selling *...For Dummies®* series has more than 19 million copies in print with translations in 28 languages. IDG Books Worldwide, through a recent joint venture with IDG's Hi-Tech Beijing, became the first U.S. publisher to publish a computer book in the People's Republic of China. In record time, IDG Books Worldwide has become the first choice for millions of readers around the world who want to learn how to better manage their businesses.

Our mission is simple: Every one of our books is designed to bring extra value and skill-building instructions to the reader. Our books are written by experts who understand and care about our readers. The knowledge base of our editorial staff comes from years of experience in publishing, education, and journalism — experience which we use to produce books for the '90s. In short, we care about books, so we attract the best people. We devote special attention to details such as audience, interior design, use of icons, and illustrations. And because we use an efficient process of authoring, editing, and desktop publishing our books electronically, we can spend more time ensuring superior content and spend less time on the technicalities of making books.

You can count on our commitment to deliver high-quality books at competitive prices on topics consumers want to read about. At IDG Books Worldwide, we value quality, and we have been delivering quality for more than 25 years. You'll find no better book on a subject than an IDG book.

John J. Kilcullen

John Kilcullen
President and CEO
IDG Books Worldwide, Inc.

IDG Books Worldwide, Inc., is a subsidiary of International Data Group, the world's largest publisher of computer-related information and the leading global provider of information services on information technology. International Data Group publishes over 235 computer publications in 67 countries. More than seventy million people read one or more International Data Group publications each month. The officers are Patrick J. McGovern, Founder and Board Chairman; Kelly Conlin, President; Jim Casella, Chief Operating Officer. International Data Group's publications include: **ARGENTINA'S** Computerworld Argentina, Infoworld Argentina; **AUSTRALIA'S** Computerworld Australia, Computer Living, Australian PC World, Australian Macworld, Network World, Mobile Business Australia, Publish!, Reseller, IDG Sources; **AUSTRIA'S** Computerwelt Oesterreich, PC Test; **BELGIUM'S** Data News (CW); **BOLIVIA'S** Computerworld; **BRAZIL'S** Computerworld, Connections, Game Power, Mundo Unix, PC World, Publish, Super Game; **BULGARIA'S** Computerworld Bulgaria, PC & Mac World Bulgaria, Network World Bulgaria; **CANADA'S** CIO Canada, Computerworld Canada, InfoCanada, Network World Canada, Reseller; **CHILE'S** Computerworld Chile, Informatica; **COLOMBIA'S** Computerworld Colombia, PC World; **COSTA RICA'S** PC World; **CZECH REPUBLIC'S** Computerworld, Elektronika, PC World; **DENMARK'S** Communications World, Computerworld Denmark, Computerworld Focus, Macintosh Produktkatalog, Macworld Danmark, PC World Danmark, PC Produktguide, Tech World, Windows World; **ECUADOR'S** PC World Ecuador; **EGYPT'S** Computerworld (CW) Middle East, PC World Middle East; **FINLAND'S** MikroPC, Tietoviikko, Tietoverkko; **FRANCE'S** Distributique, GOLDEN MAC, InfoPC, Le Guide du Monde Informatique, Le Monde Informatique, Telecoms & Reseaux; **GERMANY'S** Computerwoche, Computerwoche Focus, Computerwoche Extra, Electronic Entertainment, Gamepro, Information Management, Macwelt, Netzwelt, PC Welt, Publish, Publish; **GREECE'S** Publish & Macworld; **HONG KONG'S** Computerworld Hong Kong, PC World Hong Kong; **HUNGARY'S** Computerworld SZT, PC World; **INDIA'S** Computers & Communications; **INDONESIA'S** Info Komputer; **IRELAND'S** ComputerScope; **ISRAEL'S** Beyond Windows, Computerworld Israel, Multimedia, PC World Israel; **ITALY'S** Computerworld Italia, Lotus Magazine, Macworld Italia, Networking Italia, PC Shopping Italy, PC World Italia; **JAPAN'S** Computerworld Today, Information Systems World, Macworld Japan, Nikkei Personal Computing, SunWorld Japan, Windows World; **KENYA'S** East African Computer News; **KOREA'S** Computerworld Korea, Macworld Korea, PC World Korea; **LATIN AMERICA'S** GamePro; **MALAYSIA'S** Computerworld Malaysia, PC World Malaysia; **MEXICO'S** Compu Edicion, Compu Manufactura, Computacion/Punto de Venta, Computerworld Mexico, MacWorld, Mundo Unix, PC World, Windows; **THE NETHERLANDS'** Computer! Totaal, Computable (CW), LAN Magazine, Lotus Magazine, MacWorld; **NEW ZEALAND'S** Computer Buyer, Computerworld New Zealand, Network World, New Zealand PC World; **NIGERIA'S** PC World Africa; **NORWAY'S** Computerworld Norge, Lotusworld Norge, Macworld Norge, Maxi Data, Networld, PC World Ekspress, PC World Nettverk, PC World Norge, PC World's Produktguide, Publish& Multimedia World, Student Data, Unix World, Windowsworld; **PAKISTAN'S** PC World Pakistan; **PANAMA'S** PC World Panama; **PERU'S** Computerworld Peru, PC World; **PEOPLE'S REPUBLIC OF CHINA'S** China Computerworld, China Infoworld, China PC Info Magazine, Computer Fan, PC World China, Electronics International, Electronics Today/Multimedia World, Electronic Product World, China Network World, Software World Magazine, Telecom Product World; **PHILIPPINES'** Computerworld Philippines, PC Digest (PCW); **POLAND'S** Computerworld Poland, Computerworld Special Report, Networld, PC World/Komputer, Sunworld; **PORTUGAL'S** Cerebro/PC World, Correio Informatico/Computerworld, MacIn; **ROMANIA'S** Computerworld, PC World, Telecom Romania; **RUSSIA'S** Computerworld-Moscow, Mir - PK (PCW), Sety (Networks); **SINGAPORE'S** Computerworld Southeast Asia, PC World Singapore; **SLOVENIA'S** Monitor Magazine; **SOUTH AFRICA'S** Computer Mail (CIO), Computing S.A., Network World S.A., Software World; **SPAIN'S** Advanced Systems, Amiga World, Computerworld Espana, Communicaciones World, Macworld Espana, NeXTWORLD, Super Juegos Magazine (GamePro), PC World Espana, Publish; **SWEDEN'S** Attack, ComputerSweden, Corporate Computing, Macworld, Mikrodatorn, Natverk & Kommunikation, PC World, CAP & Design, Datalngenjoren, Maxi Data, Windows World; **SWITZERLAND'S** Computerworld Schweiz, Macworld Schweiz, PC Tip; **TAIWAN'S** Computerworld Taiwan, PC World Taiwan; **THAILAND'S** Thai Computerworld; **TURKEY'S** Computerworld Monitor, Macworld Turkiye, PC World Turkiye; **UKRAINE'S** Computerworld, Computers+Software Magazine; **UNITED KINGDOM'S** Computing/Computerworld, Connexion/Network World, Lotus Magazine, Macworld, Open Computing/Sunworld; **UNITED STATES'** Advanced Systems, AmigaWorld, Cable in the Classroom, CD Review, CIO, Computerworld, Computerworld Client/Server Journal, Digital Video, DOS World, Electronic Entertainment Magazine (E2), Federal Computer Week, Game Hits, GamePro, IDG Books Worldwide, Infoworld, Laser Event, Macworld, Maximize, Multimedia World, Network World, PC Letter, PC World, Publish, SWATPro, Video Event; **URUGUAY'S** PC World Uruguay; **VENEZUELA'S** Computerworld Venezuela, PC World; **VIETNAM'S** PC World Vietnam.

08/30/95

Dedication

To my three Js:

John, Jessie, and John-Michael.

I love you so much.

Credits

Senior Vice President and Publisher
Milissa L. Koloski

Associate Publisher
Diane Graves Steele

Brand Manager
Judith A. Taylor

Editorial Managers
Kristin A. Cocks
Mary C. Corder

Editorial Executive Assistant
Richard Graves

Editorial Assistants
Chris Collins
Stacey Holden Prince
Kevin Spencer

Acquisitions Assistant
Suki Gear

Production Director
Beth Jenkins

Supervisor of Project Coordination
Cindy L. Phipps

Supervisor of Page Layout
Kathie S. Schnorr

Pre-Press Coordinator
Steve Peake

Associate Pre-Press Coordinator
Tony Augsburger

Media/Archive Coordinator
Paul Belcastro

Project Editor
Bill Helling

Editors
Diana R. Conover
Michael Simsic

Technical Reviewer
Tommy Hann

Associate Project Coordinator
J. Tyler Connor

Production Staff
Gina Scott
Carla C. Radzikinas
Patricia R. Reynolds
Melissa D. Buddendeck
Leslie Popplewell
Dwight Ramsey
Robert Springer
Theresa Sánchez-Baker
Linda M. Boyer
Angela F. Hunckler
Mark C. Owens
Alicia Shimer
Michael Sullivan

Proofreader
Barb Potter

Indexer
Sharon Hilgenberg

Cover Design
Kavish + Kavish

Acknowledgments

I must again thank my husband. Writing a second book has been a challenge to both our parenting skills (things would be much easier if we believed in spanking) and our marriage (all-night writing sessions tend to put a crimp in your love life). John has held this family together like a tube of industrial strength superglue! I love you, Baby!

Teaching is rewarding, and this writing gig has been cool, but being a mom is the job that I love the most and is the one that gives me the most satisfaction. Jessie and John-Michael, you are my sunshine. I've always loved the quote, "Children are not things to be molded, but people to be unfolded." I'm having such fun watching both of you *unfold* and become special little people.

My parents have always been my biggest supporters. They stepped back and let me make my own mistakes and were there to celebrate all of my successes. I hope your "little corner" of the North Georgia Mountains turns out to be everything you've dreamed it would be.

I seem to have surrounded myself with extremely bright people.

Bard Williams is a computer whiz who patiently answered many a query during the writing of this book. Bard and I have forged a friendship that can't be matched. Bard, you know how I appreciate your help. I especially want to thank you for getting excited for me and with me!

The MacGod, David Pogue, also helped me through some difficult spots. I want to thank David for accepting my calls and answering every question without making me feel foolish or unworthy of his friendship and help.

Tommy Hann is a technical editor extraordinaire, and I thank him for pointing out all my glaring (and not so glaring) errors. Thanks for working with me and helping ensure a quality product.

I thank all the great software companies that provided me with products to preview or include on the CD. A special thanks goes out to Roger Wagner Publishing for putting together the great CD that comes packaged with this book. I specifically need to thank Roger Wagner for his enthusiasm and Maureen Gross for her helpful conversation and great contacts, Jeff Kelley is responsible for the artwork and programming behind the *Mac Multimedia For Teachers CD*. He deserves a whole page of praise for the incredible work he did under an extremely tight deadline. Jeff, you are a true renaissance man, and I know you will soar to places yet to be discovered in both the fields of technology and art.

A special thanks must go to Kevin Spencer and Bard Williams for the technical review that they performed on the *Mac Multimedia For Teachers CD*. Their suggestions helped make a great product even better. Kevin soon became the go-to guy for all our CD questions.

My project editor, Bill Helling, came through for me again! I requested this busy guy, and he graciously agreed to work my book into his busy schedule. Bill is a kind person, a great editor, and a dedicated dad — what a man!

I knew I'd work well with Diana Conover the minute Bill told me that she had been a teacher at one point in her professional life. Diana was at Bill's side throughout the entire editorial process, and I thank her for catching all my mistakes.

Jim Kelly is my other favorite guy within the IDG ranks. Jim believed in my ideas when I needed him most, and he's still there to listen with an open mind when I come up with crazy new ideas.

Tyler Connor and the entire production crew deserve a loud and rowdy round of applause. Incorporating photos and other difficult diagrams and screenshots into my text was a difficult task that Tyler and his staff pulled off with ease.

Angie Hunckler was especially tireless in her effort to make everything fit as well as possible within a very limited amount of space. And everybody should recognize the effort of Chris Collins in Dummies Press, because Chris had to keep track of literally hundreds of screen shots (not to mention that he also had to *print* hundreds of screen shots). Thanks for all your time and energy. I think everything looks super!

The Mighty Women of IDG get my final bow. That's right. I'm proud to say that many of the decision makers and go-getters within this powerful company are of the female persuasion: Milissa Koloski, Diane Steele, Judi Taylor, Mary Bednarek, Megg Bonar, and Suki Gear. I'm proud to be part of this "sisterhood."

(The Publisher would like to give special thanks to Patrick J. McGovern, without whom this book would not have been possible.)

Contents at a Glance

Cartoons at a Glance

By Rich Tennant

"I'm sorry, but Principal Halloran is being chased by six midgets with poison boomerangs through a maze in the dungeon of a castle. If he finds his way out and gets past the minotaur he'll call you right back; otherwise try again Thursday."

Page 41

"I failed her in Algebra but was impressed with the way she animated her equations to dance across the screen, scream like ingenas and then dissolve into a clip art image of the La Brea Tar Pits."

Page 7

NOT EVERYONE AT MEDVILLE HIGH SCHOOL EMBRACED MULTIMEDIA TEACHING WITH EQUAL PROFICIENCY.

"Multimedia is a wonderful combination of video, sound, graphics, animation, text ... ...and nightmares."

Page 187

"SO, HOW DO YOU LIKE THE NEW HIGH PERFORMANCE VIDEO CARD?"

Page 22

Principal

"I found these two in the multimedia lab morphing faculty members into farm animals."

Page 92

"IT WAS BETWEEN THAT AND NEW CLASSROOM COMPUTERS."

Page 161

"WELL! IT LOOKS LIKE SOMEONE FOUND THE 'LION'S ROAR' ON THE SOUND CONTROL PANEL."

Page 60

"The system came bundled with a CD-ROM drive, a sound card, and the developers out of work nephew."

Page 142

"Of course graphics are important to your project, Eddy, but I think it would've been better to scan a picture of your worm collection."

Page 79

NATIONAL ENQUIRER PHOTO IMAGING WORKSHOP

"Remember, Charles and Di can be pasted next to anyone but each other, and your Elvis should appear bald and slightly hunched - juke Big Foot, Brad - keep your two-headed animals in the shadows and your alien spacecrafts crisp and defined."

Page 212

Table of Contents

Foreword

As a child I always knew that my parents could play games better than I could. And as a student I never thought that I was as smart as my teachers. But that's one of the things computers have changed. It's true: a bright fourth grader can usually surpass a typical teacher's knowledge of the computer in a couple of months *after discovering the computer*. And the student will probably soon be answering some technical questions for the teacher.

Today's curious young mind discovers how to write by using a new technique — word processing. The rules and methods of the endeavor are as interesting as the nicely printed results. After a little skill development on keyboarding, young students express themselves more fully with their writing.

The students next learn how to space items on a page, for the sake of appearance, and how to choose fonts and sizes. Then come graphics. Many teachers are still impressed when students fill reports with colors and clip art. It's hard to find a student with computer access who doesn't quickly develop the ability to impress teachers with a small and simple artistic content. I even point out to my students that success in business is often related to how well one's written work appears.

This is where multimedia starts to come in. One of the big *Open House* hits is the student-created slide show that combines pictures, text, voices, music, and even video to explain a story. As crude as these shows might seem at first, they are immensely intriguing to parents — and I've personally seen how proud such shows make the students. Talk about self-esteem. Talk about confidence with computers!

Low-cost multimedia programs such as *KidPix* and *HyperStudio* make it simple for students to combine various elements of multimedia. The key word here is *simple*. Because many complex programs require so much learning and practice to do one small task, the richness of a student's multimedia project often suggests that the program that was used must be very complicated. But it turns out that creating multimedia projects these days can be as easy as dragging pictures and buttons onto a page. The result is so fun and interesting that it's no problem for teachers to encourage lots of experimentation. Almost any school subject can be translated into a multimedia presentation.

I've had opportunities to take more advanced multimedia classes with my own students, and I feel slightly embarrassed by the fact that most of them create better looking projects than I do!

Steve Wozniak

Co-founder of Apple Computer

Introduction

I can't run or jump like Super Mario, my bulletin board graphics are limited to the colors of construction paper in my closet, and my husband will quite honestly tell you that my singing voice is not one that you'll be hearing on MTV anytime soon! Yet today's children have become accustomed to these modern-day miracles and seem to expect the same level of excitement from their teachers.

We all know that a lecture on the water cycle isn't nearly as interesting as the latest video game; and even if it were, we teachers just can't seem to produce those awesome graphics and cool sound effects.

Educators across the world can rest assured that Mario will never take their place; and as of this printing, MTV hasn't entered the field of educational programming — not to say that it won't do so eventually. However, there is a viable alternative that our friends at Apple Computer have invested a lot of time and energy in — multimedia.

Why a Book on Multimedia?

The corporate heads in the computer industry across the country should have consulted teachers when they started devising their plans for multimedia. You see, we teachers have been doing multimedia all along — we just called it good teaching, and we didn't have a computer or software to help us pull it all together! That's right, my fellow educator; if you've ever used more than one approach while teaching a lesson — given a lecture, showed a filmstrip with cassette tape narration, and then maybe used written expression as a follow-up — you've done multimedia!

Multimedia, in the most basic of terms, is using more than one approach (text, sound, graphics, movies) with your computer to illustrate a point. It's a simple label that's being overused in a way that intimidates those people who aren't in the computer biz.

I guess what I'm trying to tell you is *don't fret*. You could probably teach the computer-industry executives a few things about getting a point across in a way that grabs someone's attention. You do it every day of the school year — it's your job!

My Quest

With this book, I hope to show you how naturally multimedia computing fits into the classroom environment. The educational applications are exciting and easy to assimilate into your day-to-day routine. If anything, the use of multimedia might just give you more time to do the type of teaching you long to do.

Like many other *real world* applications, multimedia in schools has a different look and feel than what you may have read or heard about. This book examines the "Multimedia Phenomena" and multimedia's uses in the field of education.

The Objectives

I've designed this book to do the following:

- ✔ explain multimedia vocabulary in teacher terms
- ✔ make the most of multimedia technology in the education setting
- ✔ help you fake your way through a few of the most popular multimedia composition programs
- ✔ give you list after list of educational multimedia resources

The Lesson Plan

I've divided the book into five parts and three appendixes, each with a specific purpose. Feel free to jump around the book and read the chapters that best apply to your situation. I think that you'll be amazed at how quickly all of the information will start to make sense to you!

Part 1 — Multi What?

In this part, you'll find all the explanations.

Chapter 1 unlocks the mystery behind all those new technical terms that apply to the wonderful world of multimedia.

In **Chapter 2**, I take all the important information from Chapter 1 and apply it to the confines of your four-walled classroom.

Your basic multimedia school-supply list can be found within the pages of **Chapter 3**. You'll appreciate the way I've broken the basic list up according to the amount of money you have to spend — who knows, you may already have most of the basics within your school!

Finally, **Chapter 4** explains the CD-ROM component of multimedia.

Part II — Sights and Sounds

Now I get into some of the fun stuff! This part deals with the variety of media that makes multimedia so exciting.

In **Chapter 5**, you learn all about the graphic elements behind multimedia. I discuss clip art, Kodak Photo CDs, drawing programs, painting programs, and much more.

Chapter 6 gives you the basics behind adding great sound components to your multimedia projects.

And **Chapter 7** delves into the exciting world of computerized video elements! That's right: You learn how to incorporate some of your skillful camcorder footage into your multimedia presentations.

Part III — Just Do It!

Some of you may turn to this section first — cut to the chase. I'd probably do the same.

In **Chapters 8 through 10**, you learn how to use the most popular multimedia composition programs in education: *KidPix Studio* and *HyperStudio*. I also show you some easy multimedia activities that you can complete with the educational staple *ClarisWorks*.

After you've learned how to use your favorite multimedia composition program, in **Chapter 11**, I lay out your game plan as well as throw in a few tips for easy planning, organization, and implementation of your multimedia pursuits.

Finally, in **Chapter 12**, I give you some specific content-area ideas for integrating your day-to-day curriculum with multimedia technology.

Part IV — Sharing with Others

I can honestly say that I've learned more from fellow classroom teachers than I ever learned in graduate school! Working with a group of open, sharing friends is truly a blessing. Sharing is especially important for those of us who know something about technology.

In **Chapter 13**, I discuss the problems and solutions involved with taking your show on the road.

In **Chapter 14**, I discuss the variety of ways you can share your presentations with the rest of the world.

Part V — The Part of Tens

I've heard that this part is a tradition with IDG Books Worldwide, Inc. Actually, I've found these chapters convenient for including those items that just didn't fit in anywhere else.

Chapters 15 through 21 hold lists and resources that you're sure to find helpful.

Appendixes

Appendix A: Here's where you'll find straightforward definitions for all the confusing multimedia terms.

Appendix B: This appendix holds pictures of every graphic contained within *HyperStudio* and *KidPix Studio*. I included these pictures as a service for you. Now if you're thinking of having your students create a presentation entitled *Holidays Around the World*, they can check this appendix to see what graphics they'll have access to and plan ahead for graphics they may need to create themselves. This section will save you (and your students) loads of time on the computer searching for the *perfect* graphic.

Appendix C: Boy, have I put together a great CD for you! This appendix gives you directions for using the *Mac Multimedia For Teachers CD*.

Conventions Used in This Book

 Teacher Approved — This icon highlights items or activities that I highly approve of and feel would be worthwhile additions to your classroom environment.

 Techno Terms — This icon brings your attention to multimedia terminology that I'll explain in easy-to-understand language.

 Heads Up — Wake up and pay attention! This is critical information. No sleeping or daydreaming allowed during this lesson.

 Learning Link — This icon points out great ways to integrate curriculum and technology.

 Try This — This icon points out some real *hands-on* learning activities. You know, the kind of stuff we do every day in our classrooms.

 On the CD — This icon indicates an item on the CD included with this book.

Part I
Multi What?

"I failed her in Algebra but was impressed with the way she animated her equations to dance across the screen, scream like hyenas and then dissolve into a clip art image of the La Brea Tar Pits."

In this part . . .

*L*et's dispel all the myths right off the bat. In this part, I'll disclose the hidden truth behind the *multi* in multimedia. I'll also explain the differences between multimedia for the general public and the educational interpretation of multimedia. Finally, I'll review your basic multimedia school supplies and CD-ROM technology.

Chapter 1

Don't Let the Terminology Scare You

In This Chapter

▶ Multimedia defined

▶ Basic supplies (an overview)

▶ Types of multimedia

▶ Digital conversion makes (almost) all things possible

▶ The "Real World"

1 don't remember the exact day that it happened, but one day, without my knowledge or consent, the library at my school began calling itself a "Media Center." This change is sweeping the country, and veteran teachers like me are having a difficult time dropping the word *library* from our vocabulary. With the addition of computers, laser disc players, satellite dishes, and cable television, the school library as we've come to know it has had a major change in both function and decor. It may seem hard to believe, but the word *library* and its counterpart, *the card catalog*, may soon be found only in our *electronic history books*.

If you're feeling like a relic from the past, don't worry. Remember that change is good — or at least that's what our principals say when they decide to move us to another classroom or grade level!

What is Multimedia?

I've always taught students to understand unknown words by breaking them down into parts. We all know that *multi* means many or more than one. And *media* simply means a variety of mediums, such as video, sound, graphics, animation, and text. In other words, if in one lesson you lecture, draw an example on the board, view a film, and then give some type of written follow-up, you are doing a *multimedia presentation*. So, you see, in the simplest of forms, all of you "really good teachers" have been doing multimedia activities for quite some time — you just haven't been doing them on a computer!

Multimedia components

The press and other very talented authors would lead you to believe that multimedia is all about having a CD-ROM drive, a few CD titles, and a great set of speakers. Just go out to your local computer store and take a look at all the prepackaged "multimedia kits" or all the computers that are called "multimedia computers" based on the simple fact that they come packaged with CD-ROM drives and speakers.

That's just not the whole story. In truth, you can create a multimedia presentation without even using a CD-ROM drive.

Multimedia is about combining sights, sounds, and interactive elements to create an experience unlike that which comes from simply reading text or idly viewing a video. And when viewed through an educator's eye, the possibilities are endless.

Let's take a brief look the components of multimedia computing:

Computers

This one's simple. If you bought this book, you already know how wonderful the Mac is, and you more than likely have a Mac or two in your school. You may not know, however, that the Mac comes out of the box ready to perform basic multimedia tasks. To add a *peripheral* (an extra piece of equipment), you simply plug a cable into the back of the Mac and load the new software. (An IBM-compatible PC usually requires some costly and difficult-to-install add-ons to become a fully functioning multimedia machine.)

With AV Macs, Apple also has the upper hand when it comes to audio visual configurations. These Macs not only allow you to import audio and video, they also allow you to export audio and video to a TV or VCR. This capability means that you can tape your multimedia production and share it with others.

Even the lowly Macintosh LCII, a computer found in a large number of today's schools, is equipped with enough components to perform basic multimedia operations. However, to be fair, I must inform you that the more RAM and hard drive space you have, the more you'll be able to accomplish in the multimedia arena. Sound and video take major amounts of memory to run and store. I provide a more detailed list of Macintosh models and capabilities in Chapter 3.

Software

The multimedia software market is growing at a rapid pace. Many of the developers are beginning to recognize the value of those of us in education, and programs are now being created that students and teachers can use to better integrate curriculum and technology. Chapters 15 and 16 have detailed lists of interactive multimedia programs and multimedia composition programs.

CD-ROM technology

As I mentioned earlier, this one's the biggie that everyone seems to reach for when they want to say that they're "into multimedia." Yeah, it's big and important — not to mention astounding! (One CD can hold 600MB of information.)

To use a CD program, you will need a CD-ROM drive, which is now standard with most new Macs. CD-ROM technology is discussed in Chapter 4.

QuickTime technology

Some people refer to QuickTime as multimedia. QuickTime is an extension in System 7 software that enables the Mac to combine text, graphics, sound, and animation into a combined digital movie (referred to as a QuickTime movie) that can be saved and imported into presentations. The movies have control bars that allow the viewer to start or stop the movie at any time. You learn more about QuickTime technology in Chapter 7.

Video

Just about every school in America now has (or should have) a video camera for student or teacher use. Through the use of QuickTime technology, you can stop showing those horribly shot "All About Our Day" videos on Open House Night and instead show a superbly created multimedia presentation including some video footage of your class along with text, still shots, graphics, and more. With the proper accessories, you can even transfer your production to a VHS tape and show it on your VCR.

Animation

Computer-generated animation is big business in Hollywood. The Mac makes it easy for students to create animated graphics for use in multimedia productions. Put simply, animation consists of many drawings (each one slightly different from the preceding one) shown one after the other to give the illusion of motion. Animated sequences may also be saved as QuickTime movies.

Scanned images

A scanner is nothing more than a magical copier. You see, a scanner *looks* like a copier, but instead of simply spitting out a poor excuse for a black-and-white reproduction of the original, a scanner creates a digital file of your image (even in color!) that can be stored either in a computer or on a disk. A scanned image of a student's drawing can be added to a text document as an illustration, or the scanned image can become part of a multimedia presentation.

Digital cameras

These cool devices look deceptively like your ordinary run-of-the-mill 35mm cameras. However, they don't use film, and you don't have to wait 24 hours for developing. You take pictures just like you would with a standard 35mm camera. However, when you're ready to view your masterpieces, you simply plug the camera into your Mac and transfer the images to your computer. (It's really easy to use!) You are then free to use the images in any of your multimedia, graphics, or word processing programs.

Photo CDs

The folks at Kodak are proud to bring you this little invention. Photos taken on your standard 35mm camera can now be developed onto a CD. This CD can then be inserted into your CD-ROM drive, and the crystal-clear images can then be used in any of your projects! At this point the process is a little pricey, but I've heard that the prices will be coming down some as Kodak begins marketing campaigns aimed at the educational community.

Tablets

No, I'm not talking about those manuscript tablets that we all had to buy as part of our yearly school supplies. A *digital tablet* is the answer to your prayers if you just can't seem to draw with a mouse. The stylus or pen works like your mouse and even plugs into the same port on your computer. Another bonus is the fact that many of these tablets enable you to trace through a sheet of paper.

Sound

Sound can be found in many forms within multimedia. The variety ranges from simple digital audio that is recorded with your Mac's microphone and then saved as a file, to sound recorded from a CD played in your CD-ROM drive (or even music played on a MIDI keyboard).

Laser discs

Laser discs never really took off in the home market like the manufacturer had hoped that they would. However, the education market has embraced the idea; and when used correctly, laser discs can be wonderful enhancements to classroom instruction. Many of the multimedia composition programs also support laser disc images and enable you to import images as well as video.

Types of multimedia

I like to break multimedia down into two categories: *interactive multimedia* and *multimedia composition* (or *authoring*).

Interactive multimedia

Interactive multimedia is easy to find and usually easy to use. In *interactive multimedia,* the user (the person sitting at the computer) controls what happens next. A good example of interactive multimedia would be *Encarta,* an award-winning CD encyclopedia. Within *Encarta,* you can choose your own route for your research. For instance, if you want to learn more about John F. Kennedy, you have the choice of reading text, watching a video, or viewing a snapshot that has a sound bite attached.

Another great example of interactive multimedia would be the electronic books (*e-books*) that Brøderbund does such a masterful job of creating.

The text in these books appears exactly as it does in its counterpart that you'd pick up in the library (a.k.a. *media center*). That's where the similarity ends. Each page of the book appears on your computer screen and is read aloud in the amusing voice of one of the characters. After the page is read, you are free to experience the hilarious sound effects and animation that occur whenever you click certain areas of the screen before turning the page. In addition, children (and adults) can move through the stories at their own pace. A recent addition to these Brøderbund titles includes video of the book's author discussing both the story you just viewed and the art of writing.

Interactive titles combine sights, sounds, graphics, text, and movies in a way that makes children want to become involved learners. The fact that they have active control over their learning is another factor that makes interactive multimedia even more appealing to students.

A list of quality multimedia CD titles is included in Chapter 15.

Multimedia composition or authoring

There are some great new *multimedia composition* programs that enable children to actually create their own interactive presentations. Until recently, this area of multimedia had been reserved for power users and programmers. These techno-heads use expensive authoring software to create interactive titles, such as those mentioned in the preceding section.

The new multimedia composition programs that I cover in this book don't require the complicated scripting that some of the higher-end development programs require and are relatively easy to understand. Some programs such as *KidPix2, KidPix Studio, Amazing Animation, Imagination Express,* and *Multimedia Workshop* enable students to create slide shows that appear on the computer's screen. The slides can contain text, cool graphics, sound, and even animation!

Other programs such as *HyperStudio* and *HyperCard* enable students to create buttons on cards, buttons that can be programmed (very simply) to take users to another *card* (screen) in the *stack* (a group of cards). This process enables students to become mini-programmers and also gives viewers control over their own learning; viewers simply click the button that corresponds to the direction they want to take their learning.

Digital Conversion Makes the Magic

If you're anything like me, when I first read about all the cool *stuff* you can use with multimedia computing, I kept thinking, "How do they do that?" The answer is digitizing.

To put it simply, *digitizing* involves converting different types of media into something the computer can understand. Synthesized sound and scanned graphics were the first components to be easily digitized for the computer. The most recent elements to be mastered were animation, video, and true sound control. Being able to involve and control all of these elements through a computer is what makes creating multimedia a truly incredible feat that is now being accomplished in the home, in business, and at school.

Multimedia in the "Real World"

In my first book, *Macs For Teachers* (IDG Books Worldwide, 1995), I spent a good deal of time pointing out the differences between the educational and *real world* applications. I'm pleased to say that, when it comes to multimedia, the business and educational uses seem to complement each other. Many of the business uses for multimedia have inspired the way I use multimedia in the school.

In the real world, advertisers use multimedia components to pitch their products. The entertainment industry has made a fortune creating programs labeled *edutainment* that involve varying degrees of multimedia components. Marketing executives use multimedia presentations to demonstrate new products or ideas. And we can't forget the education market, which itself is a form of business. As you can see, many of these same ideas can be used to enhance learning of a particular subject or skill.

Chapter 2
Multimedia Goes to School

. . . .

. . . .

*T*he term *multimedia* is being thrown around educational circles the way *whole language* was a few years back. Many teachers and administrators use the term freely but, when pressed for a good definition, would probably have a hard time explaining just what whole language really is. Many of us have come to understand and embrace the ideas behind whole language. And now that you've wisely chosen to purchase this book, you will (I hope) become the sage in your school who informs the masses on the benefits and uses of multimedia in the school setting.

Technology Meets Creativity

Technology has suffered from a cold and passive reputation. Many people have long believed that the use of computer technology in education involves nothing more than a lot of one-on-one time with a computer screen. This theory worries parents as well as teachers. Sure, computers could teach, but what would happen to our students' social skills? And (more importantly) what would eventually become of our jobs as teachers?

Put your fears to rest, dear friends. Multimedia allows the inspired force of creativity (which sometimes requires human interaction and a little teacher guidance) to merge and meld with the oh-so-powerful force of technology. That's right: In order to create multimedia presentations, students must first know what they want their presentations to cover and then must go through some detailed planning and research before they ever sit in front of a computer. Many multimedia projects are created by groups or pairs of students; the planning, research, and progress must be monitored by a teacher, thus leaving students' social skills and our jobs intact.

Authentic Assessment: Showing What You Know

I wasn't a straight-A student in school. When I studied, I studied hard. Learning wasn't easy for me, and nothing made me angrier than finishing a test and realizing that the teacher hadn't asked me about half of the stuff I'd studied.

As a teacher, I now see things from the other side. How do you create a test that's neither too long *nor* too simple, yet somehow covers all the information you've taught? This dilemma isn't an easy one to overcome.

Through the use of *authentic assessment,* or allowing students to *show what they know,* you can attempt to meet the needs of each student. Multimedia presentations fit wonderfully into this idea of allowing children to express their knowledge in a way that best suits their individual learning style.

Educational researcher Howard Gardner laid the groundwork for authentic assessment when he identified seven areas of intelligence within all humans: logical/mathematical, verbal/linguistic, musical, bodily/kinesthetic, spatial, interpersonal, and intrapersonal. We all have varying degrees of intelligence in each of these areas.

Most of us feel strongly about our intelligence in one or more of these areas, and we also tend to know our own weak areas. (In my case, it's musical. I can't sing!) However, in schools we tend to teach and test with our focus mainly on the areas of logical/mathematical (math, science, computation) and verbal/linguistic (grammar, creative writing, language arts). That focus leaves many students with intelligence that we teachers have not allowed them to express.

Because the potential impact for all children is incredible, many school systems have adopted the goals of authentic assessment and are restructuring both their teaching and testing practices.

Multimedia's role

Because multimedia production can involve a variety of resources — music, research, drawing, photography, charts, graphs, layout, video, individual work, and group work — there is a good likelihood that a teacher can use multimedia projects in an attempt to meet each student's learning style.

Accomplishing this goal is not an easy feat . . . but, then again, neither is creating a test that covers "just the right amount" of a subject! However, the benefits — engaged learners, knowledge that stays with the students because they had a role in its learning, pride in the end product, and a teaching environment that is stimulating and rewarding — all add up to make authentic assessment a worthwhile pursuit.

Software for authentic assessment

Here are a few of my favorite programs for use in the area of authentic assessment. Contact Educational Resources (800-624-2926), one of my favorite educational software providers, for current prices and availability of site licenses or lab packs.

- ✔ *HyperStudio* (Roger Wagner Productions, $109.95, upper elementary to adult)

- ✔ *KidPix Studio* (Brøderbund, $55.95, elementary to middle school)

- ✔ *KidPix2* (Brøderbund, $49.95, elementary)

- ✔ *Multimedia Workshop* (Davidson, $84.95, middle school to high school)

- ✔ *ClarisWorks* (Claris, $130.00, elementary to adult)

What it looks like

You can tailor your authentic assessment multimedia projects to suit your teaching style, your time frame, and the resources that your school has available for you. Recently, for example, I worked with a group of fifth graders to complete a five-week study on World War II.

The class was divided into groups of three. Each group was assigned a specific aspect of this time period (concentration camps, Hitler's rise to power, the atomic bomb) to research. After getting together all their facts, the students of each group decided what to include on each screen of their presentation and created a storyboard. Finally, each group worked at the computer to create a presentation, which eventually became part of the World War II production.

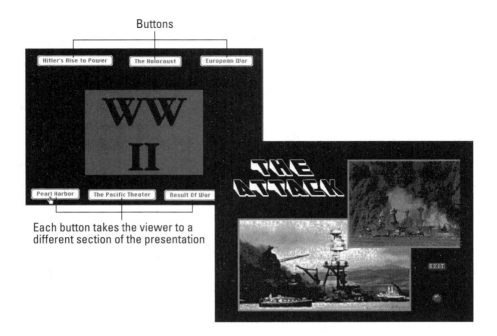

Each button takes the viewer to a different section of the presentation

This is just one example of a project to give you an idea of what can be done with authentic assessment. In Chapters 13 and 14, I provide tons of ideas for curriculum integration (and planning tips), as well as step-by-step instructions for some of the most popular authentic assessment software.

Portfolio Assessment: Keeping Track of It All

Portfolios, portfolios, portfolios. Everybody's talking about them, yet very few teachers do a good job creating or keeping up with them.

It's a great idea to use portfolios of work samples and self-evaluations of your students' work to show their growth through the year. I guess if I were single and childless, I might have the time to keep portfolios of my students; but then again, I can think of a lot of other things that I'd probably be doing if I were single and childless!

Software solutions

Our software-creating friends have come up with some pretty incredible solutions that take the time and drudgery out of portfolios. I'm mentioning these solutions to you now because they all contain such multimedia components as the capability to include sound, QuickTime movies, and scanned images in a child's portfolio.

Three companies provide software programs for portfolio assessment:

- ✔ **Scholastic's Electronic Portfolio** (Scholastic, $295, all grades, site license available)
- ✔ **The Grady Profile** (Aurbach & Associates, $134, all grades, site license available)
- ✔ **The Portfolio Assessment Kit** (SuperSchool Software, $199, all grades, site license available)

Tell them what they'll get, Michelle

What makes these programs worthy of mention in this book is that they all integrate different forms of media to give the teacher, parent, or student an overall look at the student's individual performance for a year (or more).

The text aspects of these programs include the capability to maintain student data with ease. Forget about filling out those 3×5 index cards on registration day. Just have each parent fill out an electronic information card for you!

![Student Stack screen showing a student information form with Name: Demo-Student, Ann; Student ID: 123-45-6789; Class: 95; Sex: Female; Birthdate: 2/24/81; Enrolled: 9/4/85; Ethnic: Asian checked; Year: 93-94; Grade: 7; Teacher: Miss Nelson; Attendance: 0 days missed as of 3/1/94; Scholastic History listing 1st Place in Science Fair (Gd. 4, Yr. 90) and 2nd place in spelling bee (Gd. 6, Yr. 92)]

Each program has capabilities that enable you to scan in student work samples (no more bulging hanging files) and add audio of the student discussing the work (or reading it aloud). You can also import QuickTime video footage of the student giving a speech or performing in a play (if your Mac has Video In and Audio In ports).

The Portfolio Assessment Kit contains a neat journal feature. This area allows students to make daily (or weekly) journal entries; and the area also has a space for keeping track of creative writing ideas as well as a monthly calendar/ planning section and a phone directory. The kids can even choose what type of background they want for their journal screen (a race car, a floral design, and so on).

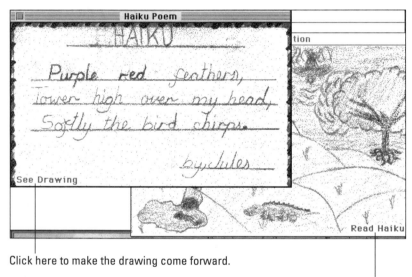

Click here to make the drawing come forward.

Click here to hear the poem read.

And if all that isn't enough (don't I sound like a salesperson?), Scholastic even throws in a presentation program that enables you to compile highlights from a student's school year into a program that can be transferred to a VHS videotape if your Mac has AV capabilities or you have a presentation system. (See Chapter 14 for more details.)

Wow! Have I convinced you?

Take a peek at the demo versions of *The Grady Profile* and *Scholastic's Electronic Portfolio* on the *Mac Multimedia For Teachers CD*.

Limitations

In the newspaper ads, this part would probably be in fine print: All these amazing feats require major memory.

Although the capability to include scanned images, QuickTime movies, and sound is a wonderful plus, the storage requirements for such files are overwhelming. You would need one file for each child in your class! If an entire school adopted this concept, I'm not sure how all the information would be stored if you want to use the programs in the way that they were intended to be used. Each teacher would need access to some type of external storage device or a WORM drive that writes information onto a CD like the folks at Kodak do with the photo CDs (see Chapter 4).

I also feel very strongly about continuity issues. If I spend a whole year compiling all this neat data on each child in my third-grade classroom, I certainly hope that the data would be carried over by the next year's teacher.

In my heart, I see these portfolio assessment programs playing a big role in the future. I think that whole school systems will eventually adopt this concept. With technology prices going down, I also see teachers eventually being provided with all the necessary hardware that will allow them to take advantage of all the cool features each program offers.

Student Power

The world today is very different than it was while you and I were growing up. I believe that self-confidence and decision-making skills will play a crucial role in the lives of today's young people.

Authentic assessment projects help students by not only requiring research but by also requiring planning, using complex thought processes, working with others, preparing information to be seen by others, and developing group social skills.

Portfolio assessment allows students to be judged against themselves (not others), instills a sense of pride in their work, and allows them to see personal growth.

If multimedia technology in the school does nothing more than instill feelings of pride, accomplishment, and self-worth, it will have done more than enough. For, you see, I believe that after you've accomplished those feats, the rest will come with ease!

Chapter 3

School Supplies

*W*hen I first began teaching, I would produce elaborately detailed lists of school supplies that I expected students to bring on the first day of school. Each year the list got shorter and shorter as I realized that I could do without some of the items — except for the mandatory box of tissues. I found that by starting with a small list and then asking for items as I needed them (a bottle of vinegar for our erupting volcanoes; colored copy paper for our published stories), parents were more than willing to provide what I needed with very little opposition.

It's the same way with multimedia computing. After reading this chapter, you're probably going to make one of those long supply lists for your principal or school system administrators. However, like me, you're going to have to scale down your list, make the best of what you have, and then prove to them that you deserve more!

Computers

Don't believe *everything* you read about multimedia computing. You don't need the newest, most expensive Mac in order to perform basic multimedia tasks — you don't even need a CD-ROM drive (although the added benefits of having a CD-ROM drive are great).

Having said that, I do admit that, in this case, bigger is better. When your school can afford to upgrade, it should buy the biggest and the best Mac its budget allows. Table 3-1 shows the current Mac models and their configurations.

Take a look at what your school or you currently own and then read on.

Table 3-1	Macs Commonly Found in Schools			
Model	*RAM*	*Internal CD*	*Video In & Out*	*Processor*
LCII	2 or 4 MB	No	No	68030 at 16MHz
LCIII	4MB	No	No	68030 at 25 MHz
LC 475	4MB	No	No	680LC40 at 25 MHz
LC520	5MB	Yes	No	68030 at 25 MHz
LC550	4MB	Yes	No	68030 at 33 MHz
LC575	4 or 8 MB	Yes	No	68040 at 33 MHz
5200 LC	8MB	Yes	Optional	PowerPC 603 at 75 MHz
6100/60	8MB	Yes	Optional	PowerPC 60 at 60 or 66 MHz
6100/60 AV	8MB	Yes	Yes	PowerPC 60 at 60 or 66 MHz

Computer Terminology Refresher

Here are a few terms you may want to be familiar with:

AV configuration: Built-in multimedia capabilities, including the capabilities to record video directly into the computer and export sound and video to an outside unit such as a TV or VCR.

Central processing unit (CPU): Controls how fast and how complex your computer runs. The processor numbers usually start with 68 and end with numbers like 030 or 040. The higher the number, the better. Most new machines are PowerPC based.

GB: The abbreviation for gigabyte. One gigabyte equals equals 1,024 megabytes. Most new multimedia Macs come with at least a 1GB hard drive.

Hard drive (hard disk): Where you store information within your computer. A hard disk is like a giant floppy disk that holds all your files and programs. You can also purchase external hard drives for your use in case you fill up the hard drive on your computer. The information on the hard drive (hard disk) is there all the time (even while your computer is turned off). When working with multimedia, a large hard drive is a valuable asset. Some schools also purchase a file server to handle the memory requirements of a Mac lab. QuickTime videos, scanned images, color graphics, and sound bites each take up huge amounts of hard-drive space.

Hard-drive capacity: The amount of data in the form of megabytes (MB) or gigabytes (GB) that a hard drive can store. You want to have big numbers here!

MB: The abbreviation for megabyte. One megabyte equals 1,024K (kilobytes). A kilobyte is a size measurement for computer information. A floppy disk usually holds from 800 to 1,400 kilobytes of information or data.

MHz: Refers to clock speed; determines the amount of information the processor can address at one time. The higher the clock speed, the more efficient the processor can process information.

NTSC Video Output: Enables your Mac to output a video signal to a TV.

Power Macintosh: A Mac that contains the PowerPC chip. These processors are the fastest made for Macs today.

RAM: When people talk about memory, this is the number they refer to. To check the amount of memory your Mac model has, choose About This Macintosh from the menu. This memory exists only while your Mac is running. RAM is expensive and limited. The more RAM your computer has, the smoother multimedia programs run.

SCSI devices: Computer "extras" (also known as "the fun stuff"), such as scanners, printers, and external hard drives.

System software (MacOS): The software that makes a Mac a Mac. It tells the computer how to act and allows the Mac to communicate information among different parts of the computer and its peripherals (CD drives, modems, scanners). The latest version of system software is 7.5. New system software is due out sometime in 1996. Most of the current software programs require System 7 or higher.

Video capture: What happens when you record video to your hard drive.

VRAM (Video RAM): Memory that is put aside for storing the images on your monitor. This determines how many colors that you can display on your monitor and how big your monitor can be.

Robinette's Basic Supply Lists

Okay, folks. Here it is in black and white. I'm giving you your supply list, and it's up to you to find the money. Buy what you can afford and then build your inventory as money becomes available.

Minimal

80MB hard drive
4MB RAM
68030 processor
System 7.0

Multimedia software you can use: *KidPix2* or *KidPix with KidPix Companion, Monstrous Media Kid* (limited), *Microsoft Fine Artist, Claris Amazing Animation, HyperStudio* (limited).

Better

250MB hard drive
8MB RAM
68040 processor
CD-ROM drive (double-speed)
System 7.0 or higher

Multimedia software you can use (in addition to software previously listed): *HyperStudio* (fully functioning), *Monstrous Media Kid* (fully functional), *Multimedia Workshop, Aldus Persuasion,* most paint or drawing programs, most interactive encyclopedias, and other interactive CDs.

Best

AV configuration
500MB (or higher) hard drive
16MB (or higher) RAM
PowerPC processor
CD-ROM drive (quad speed)
System 7.5
external hard drive

Multimedia software you can use (in addition to software previously listed): Just about anything you'd like to try!

Upgrading Your School Computers: How and When

Now that you've located your computer on the table at the beginning of this chapter and read through the supply lists, you're probably painfully aware of your limitations (both technologically and financially) and have already envisioned the ideal setup. Allow me now to throw some more information at you. Upgrading your school computers is an option to enhance your computers in an effort to gain better performance.

How?

You can upgrade your computer in a number of different ways. The three that I describe are in order of cost, from lowest to highest. Most of these upgrades can be ordered through reputable mail-order catalogs from companies such as MacWarehouse (800-255-6227). Talk to colleagues and professionals before making a call: mail-order people are nice and helpful, but remember that they are also *sales*people. Most of the companies offer substantial educational discounts for some products. If you don't know what you need or what enhancements are compatible with your computer, don't worry; the folks at the other end of the line are very knowledgeable and ready to help.

Installation of most of these components is easy to do yourself. The technicians in my school system charge $65 per computer to install memory (RAM). When I recently installed 4MB of RAM, I was shocked when I realized how simple the operation actually was! The technician at MacWarehouse even stayed on the phone and talked me through the whole process. Although internal differences in computers do exist, the instructions that come with components from MacWarehouse address each computer and do a fine job of providing installation information.

Add more RAM

As quickly as possible, you need to acquire more RAM. Yes, you can do basic *stuff* with as little as 4MB of RAM and a measly 80MB hard drive. However, your thirst for more will soon have you begging the PTA for one of the new Power Macs with AV capabilities.

The more RAM you have in your computer, the faster your programs run. Most of the stuff you find in the area of multimedia computing is huge and requires tons of RAM (over 4MB) to run smoothly — and it can be very frustrating to children and adults when things run slow or choppy.

RAM looks like a little piece of silicon bacon — really. And it's not called RAM until it's functioning in your computer. When it's in your hand looking like a strip of silicon bacon, it's called a *SIMM,* which stands for Single Inline Memory Module. (And here's something for you: New computers use something called DIMM.) Go figure!

Buy as much RAM as your computer can accommodate and your pocketbook can afford.

Buy an external hard drive

An external hard drive won't do much to help your computer do a better job running some of the neat multimedia programs that you want to create or experience. It will, however, give you a place to store some of the large multimedia files (QuickTime video, graphics, sound, and so on) that take up large amounts of space on your computer's internal hard drive. External hard drives are also handy to use when you want to take your wonderful multimedia presentations on the road and share them with other schools or community members (see Chapter 13).

Increase the speed

Kids thrive on speed — they seem to go everywhere fast. I think that my two-year-old went straight from crawling to running. Computers seem to have done the same thing. It seems as though we went from the horribly slow Apple IICs right to the Power Macs that fly effortlessly through every task they are presented.

Once again, this solution can be found under the heading of *accelerator cards* within the catalog pages of MacWarehouse or any of the other reputable mail-order houses listed in Chapter 20. Installing one of these cards makes your computer run faster, thus decreasing the amount of time it takes to process some of the more time-consuming multimedia tasks. Accelerator cards are a little more costly than RAM but are just as easy to install. Accelerator cards are usually installed in one of your computer's NuBus or PDS slots.

When?

This is a difficult question. Unlike the home multimedia enthusiast who can spend money updating a single computer, schools need big bucks to upgrade either a lab full of computers or the computers that might be sitting in every classroom.

When and where to start are decisions that often prove to be difficult to make. In my school system, we've opted to leave most of the older computers alone and to dedicate all future technology dollars to the purchase of computers that are up-to-speed and ready for multimedia upgrades. Until you can afford new computers, you may want to try the ideas listed under "One Powerful Computer Can Make a Difference" later in this chapter.

If your school system is not ready to commit future dollars towards technology, but *you* are ready to take the multimedia plunge in a big way, you might want to seriously consider a few of the upgrade options on a limited number of computers.

One Powerful Computer Can Make a Difference

It's a little overwhelming to think about all the components that go into multimedia computing. Most schools don't have the money to purchase enough equipment to meet the needs of every classroom. My advice is to start small, work with what you have, and prioritize your *wish list*. Then, as money becomes available, you'll eventually be able to get the multimedia setup of your dreams.

Last year — thanks to lottery dollars — my school was able to purchase a Power Mac 6100/AV. It was like a dream come true! Suddenly, I was able to accomplish incredible multimedia feats with students. "What!" you exclaim. "How did one computer drastically alter the multimedia atmosphere of a school with more than 1,000 students?"

Most of the work on multimedia projects — research, planning, entering text, adding some graphics, and sound work — is done on our lowly LCIIs or Mac 520s. The students save their work to high-density (HD) disks. When everything but the video, scanned images, or extensive sound has been created, the students sign up to work with me in small groups, and we use the Power Mac to pull the whole creation together. Because we have an AV Mac (which allows me to export the production to a TV screen that is connected to a VCR), I can then copy the production onto a videotape and share it with the entire school via closed-circuit television.

We've decided to create a small multimedia lab next year. With a total of eight computers, a scanner, a TV/VCR combo, a digital camera, a video camera, and our closed-circuit TV capabilities, I'm feeling very hopeful about my school's multimedia capabilities in the upcoming years. And it all started with just one Power Mac!

The basic supply list information I've provided in this chapter will get you started in multimedia. Later in the book, you can read about some of the "toys" that are great additions and can greatly enhance your multimedia productions. If you're really curious, Deke McClelland (the Mac multimedia guru) goes into much more detail on these subjects in *Mac Multimedia & CD-ROMs For Dummies* (IDG Books Worldwide, 1995).

Buy high-quality, high-density disks

In my school district, it's possible to buy computer disks through my school system's warehouse at ridiculously low prices. At first, it Iseemed really incredible to be able to buy a box of 10 disks for $2.00; many teachers (including myself) ordered multiple boxes with our supply money. However, most of the boxes that I ordered sit unopened in my standard-issue gray metal cabinet and will probably remain there for some time.

You see, that old phrase your momma used to use, "If it seems too good to be true, it probably is," pertains to such purchases.

The first thing that you need to know about discounted bulk supplies of disks is that these disks are usually created with lower-quality materials that may lead to corrupted files if the disks aren't handled with care. The second thing is that these disks are usually very small in the memory department (usually only about 800K) — not a good thing when a single QuickTime movie or sound clip may need more space than the disk has available.

For multimedia, you want to buy high-quality, high-density disks. Look for this symbol on the box:

You won't be able to save whole multimedia productions even on an HD disk. However, high-density disks come in handy when you need to work with students on different computers in different locations and then need to compile a lot of smaller parts into one incredible multimedia whole! Another possiblity is to buy a file server for your school.

See Chapter 13 for more information on storing entire presentations.

You'll be glad that you took this advice the first time a child's file is corrupted or you've got a great piece of a presentation that won't fit onto the low-density disk you have. Believe me, it happens!

Now don't get me wrong; low-density disks aren't useless; they are fine for simple word processing files and some simple graphics applications. I'll probably send my stock of disks down to our productivity lab and let the kids use them to save their *ClarisWorks* documents.

Chapter 4
The Role of CD-ROM Technology

· ·

In This Chapter

▶ CD-ROM defined

▶ How it works

▶ CD misconceptions and limitations

▶ Ideas for CD use within the school

▶ Kids today have it easy

▶ News on the CD horizon

▶ Just thought you'd like to know

· ·

*B*y now, just about everyone in the United States of America either owns a compact disc (CD) player or has at least seen a CD. I remember when audio CDs first hit the market — I thought there would be no need for me to buy any because I already had everything I'd ever want on my old LPs.

Those thoughts changed the minute I heard the CD version of the Eagles' *Hotel California* album. I was so fired up that I taught a lesson on changes in technology. I even brought in a few of my favorite 45s, albums, cassettes, and even some old eight-track tapes that I played in my first car (a white AMC Gremlin).

What's the Big Deal?

CD-ROM technology is a *major* deal. Computer technology grows in leaps and bounds every day. The number of computer programs and computer users seems to be growing just as quickly. CD-ROM discs are the answer to these growing pains.

Because CD-ROM discs can't be altered by magnetic fields, they are easy to store and transport. They are also cheap to produce and encode. And above all, they hold tons-of-information — 600MB! That's more room than can be found on the average computer's hard drive.

The Move to CDs

Recent trends have shown that many software companies are putting their software titles on CD-ROM discs rather than transporting them on the traditional floppy disks. Many of the programs aren't intended to be run from the CD each time they are used. Placing a program on one CD simply makes installation of the program on your hard drive easier because it eliminates the need to switch back and forth between four or five disks during installation. The CDs are also easier to store than a pile of disks, and they take up less space. **Please note:** Most of the companies still offer disk versions of the same software for those folks who still don't own CD-ROM drives.

The amount of storage space on a CD-ROM disc makes it possible for software manufacturers to package both IBM and Mac versions of software on one CD.

CD-ROM Explained

I'm willing to wager that, if you've purchased this book, you probably have a CD-ROM drive attached to your home computer or a computer that you now use at school. Apple is so convinced of the value of CD-ROMs that they've decided to make CD-ROM drives standard issue with most of their new computers.

CD stands for *compact disc*. ROM stands for *read-only memory*. Read-only memory means that you can only read, see, or hear what's on the CD. You can't make any changes to the contents of the CD. Most CD-ROM drives can read a variety of different CD types including Kodak Photo CDs and audio CDs.

How it works

The information on a CD isn't recorded by using a magnetic coating such as that found on your hard disk or your 3.5-inch floppies. Instead, the information is stamped into smooth areas *(lands)* and depressed areas *(pits)*. After a disc has been stamped with its positive and negative areas, the information stamped onto it can't be changed or altered. A laser light then scans the disc. The patterns created by reflected light are interpreted as binary information that's reported to the computer. All of this information is eventually (don't ask me how) turned into the sights and sounds that you experience.

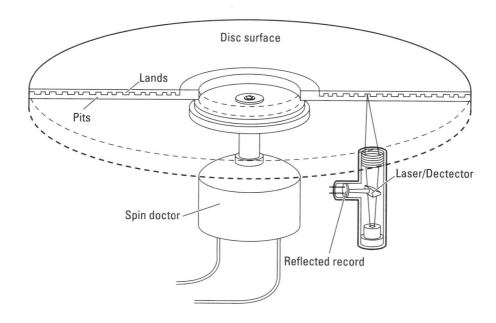

Disc surface

Lands

Pits

Laser/Dectector

Spin doctor

Reflected record

CD-ROM drive speed

Your boom box and stereo play CDs at *single speed*. CD-ROM drives now come in *double speed, triple speed,* and *quad speed*. I suggest that you equip your computers with at least a double-speed drive. I've seen some models selling for as little as $149.

The faster your CD-ROM drive, the better your computer can run the programs contained on the CD.

CD-ROM Technology in the School Setting

Pros and cons to using CDs in the school setting exist. In the wonderful world of education, money is always a problem. If you can somehow get past that hurdle, I'd have no problem telling you to "go for it!" However, as you can see, money is the root of all CD evil.

CD-ROM technology pros:

- ✔ CD-ROM programs are wonderfully rich, colorful, and exciting.

- ✔ The programs are full of information that's usually arranged in a very appealing and easy-to-understand manner.

- ✔ Many of the programs serve as great research tools that not only put written information at a student's fingertips but also include sound, graphics, and even movies. What a wonderful way to get kids excited about the research process!

CD-ROM technology cons:

- ✔ CD-ROM programs are usually more expensive.

- ✔ CD-ROM programs can't be used in a network without costly special server software. Otherwise, you must have a copy of a CD for each computer. With floppy-based software, you can take advantage of a variety of pricing options (site license, lab packs, and so on). In other words, CD-ROM technology can be costly in the lab setting. However, some companies do offer discounts for bulk purchases of CD titles.

- ✔ Most schools started purchasing computers in the days of the LCIIs and LCIIIs. They are great little machines, although neither of these models of computers has a built-in CD-ROM drive or the RAM capability that allows the best possible performance from a CD. Adding memory and CD-ROM drives is a costly option.

What Should You Do?

Gosh, I don't know whether there is an answer. A number of options are available, none of which make me totally happy. I just wish each school could be given the technological hardware and money needed to take advantage of all the cool stuff that's out there.

By all means, buy CD-ROMs. Find ways to be creative with their use. (Of course, I'd like every teacher to have a classroom full of computers or at least one computer with a CD-ROM drive and a vast library of CD titles.)

I know: reality, reality, reality.

Here are two viable options for you to try within your own school:

✔ Add CD-ROM drives to a small group of computers in your media center. Or as you purchase new computers with internal CD-ROM drives, place those computers in the media center and use this "Cluster o' ROM" as a research area.

We use this idea in my school, and it really works well: We keep a different research CD title in each computer in the media center. The students come in on their own, or in small groups, to do research. (We also use this area to do small-group instruction on *HyperStudio*.)

✔ Have one computer (or more) with a CD-ROM drive per grade level. Housing the computer on a rolling cart and creating a schedule for sharing it among the teachers makes access to CD-ROM technology for all students (at some point, hopefully) easy.

It would be nice to have one copy of each CD title for every grade level. However, keeping the CDs in the media center for checkout works just as well.

Well, those are my opinions. Write and tell me about your innovative uses of CD-ROM titles in your schools. I've always gotten some of my best teaching ideas from peers.

Where's the Card Catalog?

I never imagined that I'd hear myself utter these words, but . . . "Today's kids have it easy." Students have every bit of knowledge they could ever need available on CDs. With a good encyclopedia on CD, a student can get a quote for a report, find the name of California's state flower, and even see video footage of a speech given by Martin Luther King, Jr.

Because CDs can hold so much information, they are the perfect medium for reference software. Over the past five years, reference CDs have exploded onto the market, and each year the titles become even more sophisticated.

Reference CDs can be divided into two categories: *general learning* and *specific learning*. In the general-learning CD category, you can find the basics: dictionaries, thesauruses, encyclopedias, and an atlas or two. The specific-learning CDs target one area or topic of learning, such as the ocean, and contain a vast array of information on that individual subject. Specific-learning CDs often include fun activities that actually take the learner into the subject and involve many interactive aspects in the research process — kinda like what we teachers call "hands-on learning activities."

Good reference CDs should be easier to use than their hardcover counterparts. In the case of general-learning software, the ease of use is immediately evident — every volume of an encyclopedia is on one CD, and the articles are cross-referenced for easy access to related information.

A good reference CD should also be easy to use, and producers of dated material should provide a yearly upgrade at a nominal fee.

Chapter 17 gives the names and descriptions of some of my favorite CD titles. I've broken this list down according to subject area and grade level.

Media Clips Available on CD

This stuff is really fun! You can buy CDs that are full of nothing but photos, clip art, maps, animation, QuickTime movies, music clips, sound effects, or a combination of any of the above-listed items. Most of the discs are royalty-free, which means you don't have to worry about copyright infringement if your multimedia presentation wins some type of national competition. The only time you may need to read the fine print is if you plan to create a production and sell it for profit.

Media clip CDs are wonderful resources for students. I'd like to see more companies tailoring clip media for educational use. Most of the titles on the market today are primarily for business users (big surprise); yet you will still find plenty of clips to meet your needs.

Latest and Greatest News on the CD Frontier

I recently noticed recordable CDs *(CD-Rs)* for sale in some of my mail-order catalogs and became very excited. These CDs use the same technology as the Kodak Photo CD. My hopes were quickly dashed when I was told that these CDs required special drives in order to record. These drives are called *WORM* (write once, read many) *drives,* and they cost about $2,000 each (not in *my* school's immediate budget). You can write on a track of the CD once, but you can read (or play) that track as often as you'd like.

Eventually, I'm sure, like all technology, the price of CD-Rs and WORM drives will come down, and every school will own these neat devices. I think CD-Rs would be an ideal way to store student portfolio records, archives of student-created multimedia, or even school "electronic yearbooks."

Stuff Teachers Need to Know

So, now you know more than you probably ever wanted to know about CDs, how they work, and what's so great about them. Now I get down to brass tacks. I'm going to tell you the stuff you *need* to know. This next section is like your first day working at a new school. They've given you your teacher's editions, assigned you to a grade level, given you a class list, and shown you your new classroom; and you can't wait for everyone to leave you alone so that you can explore and find out the answers to the important stuff such as, how far it is from your new classroom to the rest room and whether the trip can be made in less than two minutes!

Caddy, please!

When CDs first came out, I remember hearing how incredibly resilient they were. The people making these claims had never worked in *my* school!

CD-ROM drives come in two styles: caddy and caddy-less (tray-loading). A CD *caddy* is a container that protects the CD. A caddy costs about $5 and looks a great deal like the case the CD was originally packaged in. The only difference between the original case and a caddy is that the caddy contains a strip of metal that slides back to reveal the surface of the CD after it has been placed in the CD-ROM drive. Some older Macs and CD-ROM drives require a CD to be encased in a caddy before you can insert the CD into the CD-ROM drive and access information. Other (newer) Macs and CD-ROM drives allow you to put the naked CD right into a pop-out tray; and then, with a push of a button, the computer sucks the CD right in.

As a teacher in a classroom full of 25 or more students, I prefer to keep the CDs in a caddy. We all love kids. But face it — they just aren't careful sometimes (major revelation, right?). By keeping the CDs in caddies, I keep the discs away from their precious fingers and thus extend the life of the CDs.

I prefer to keep the caddy-less CD-ROM computers in the media center (where assistance with CD insertion is more readily available) and have the caddy-requiring systems out in the classrooms. My school purchased enough caddies to house each CD used in the classrooms in order to prevent anyone from ever having to touch the CD itself.

Because most of Apple's newer Macs are caddy-less, I'm going to have to do some training on the care and feeding of CDs. Check out "Grunge and dust are bad things" later in this chapter for details.

You're a jewel!

Those frustrating, fragile, hard-to-open boxes that CDs come packaged in are called *jewel cases*. I hate them. They break the first time you drop them, and even frequent CD users sometimes swear while trying to open them.

I also think that jewel cases are far too similar in size and shape to the CD caddies I just discussed. I guess that's the reason one teacher at my school (who shall remain anonymous) shoved the jewel case inside the CD-ROM drive of a brand new computer, and we had to pay a hefty technician's bill to repair the damage. Don't do this!

I suggest buying a CD caddy for each of your CDs and throwing away the jewel cases. A number of other storage possibilities are available on the market — check the MacWarehouse catalog (800-255-6227) for some cool storage options.

Grunge and dust are bad things

As the kids would say, "No, duh." But when was the last time the school janitor came down to your classroom and offered to dust the bookcases and chalkboard ledge? And I'm sure that all the children in your classroom wash their hands after playing outside, going to the rest room, and eating lunch or a snack.

That last paragraph sounded somewhat sarcastic (okay, *very* sarcastic), but these realities are *our* realities.

I hope that the technology-type person within your school told you to keep your computer away from dust — if at this moment your classroom computer is pushed up against your chalkboard . . . move it now.

The same holds true for CDs. Grunge and dust will hinder a CD's performance. The little laser beam that reads information gets all confused when it encounters grape jelly or a speck of red Georgia clay.

Here are a few tips on cleaning and caring for your CDs:

> ✔ Never, ever, *ever* polish your CD as you would an apple from a student. Don't even be tempted to "tissue-off" the dust. The best way to clean a CD is to hold it under running water and then carefully pat it dry with a clean, dust-free cloth. For actual "chunks" of food or playground matter, I've been told that a small dot of dishwashing detergent under a great deal of room-temperature running water does the trick — just don't rub the disc.

- ✔ The plain side of the disc (the side without the name or logo) contains all the "good stuff." Be especially careful when dealing with this side.

- ✔ Some really cool people handle CDs by placing their finger through the center hole — like a kid eating those flower-shaped butter cookies. Others prefer to hold a disc by its outside edge. Either method is accepted by the American Dental Association and me.

- ✔ Try not to expose discs to extreme heat or cold. That means: Don't leave them in your classroom in Death Valley during the summer while the air conditioning is off or leave them on the seat of your flashy sports car while you take a dip in the pool at your country club.

Sometimes CDs walk away

That's right! Just like the dollar bill you know was sitting on the corner of your desk, little Susie's hair bow, and your new red pen, sometimes compact discs decide they're tired of your bulletin boards and go home with a child.

I'm making light of a very serious problem: theft. CDs aren't like traditional software programs that have disks (disks that you store in your locked closet after you've loaded the programs on your computer's hard drive) because a CD must be in the CD-ROM drive in order to run. If it's an exciting CD, within reach, and the time is right . . . there may be a student who decides to take it home.

The average CD runs around $45 or more. A CD isn't a piece of bubble gum that mom can just come to the school and replace. My whole point is that you may want to consider some type of accountability process for the CDs within your school.

At my school, the students aren't allowed to load CDs without teacher supervision, and teachers must check CD titles out from the library. I also try to get around to each classroom early in the school year to discuss the rules of computer use, proper CD handling, and the consequences of breaking school rules.

Using Your CD-ROM Drive to Play Audio CDs

Apple CD-ROM players come with a desk accessory that allows you to enjoy your favorite James Taylor CD after the last bus pulls away from the school, and you're still grading papers.

You can find the accessory listed in the menu as either Apple CD Remote or Apple CD Audio Player. After you place your Sweet Baby James CD into the CD-ROM drive, the icon appears on your desktop. However, you won't see a picture of James or even the name of the CD; the icon on your desktop just says Audio CD. Opening the Apple CD Remote or Apple CD Audio Player gives you access to the same easy-to-understand controls that you find on a standard CD player.

Neat Secrets: You can turn the volume up or down by simply pressing the up- or down-arrow keys on your keyboard. You can also use the left- and right-arrow keys to move through the music tracks.

Now that I've unmasked the mystery behind CD-ROM, read on and find out all about the secrets behind adding tons of sights and sounds to your multimedia pursuits.

Part II
Sights and Sounds

The 5th Wave   By Rich Tennant

"I'm sorry, but Principal Halloran is being chased by six midgets with poison boomerangs through a maze in the dungeon of a castle. If he finds his way out and gets past the minotaur he'll call you right back; otherwise try again Thursday."

In this part . . .

Let's face it: You are in direct competition with Super Mario and MTV. I sometimes feel that, if I could rap my social studies lesson or had flashing lights and taped applause for correct answers, I just might be able to hold the attention of my entire class for at least 15 minutes.

In this part, I'm going to show you some great multimedia components that just might give Super Mario a run for his money. You'll learn all about enhancing your computer's function through the use of CD-ROM technology, VCRs, camcorders, laser discs, and sound.

When do we get to go *outside*? Do I *have* to do this? It's due *when*? We deal with those questions on a daily basis. Don't forget that your students are just kids, and a major part of their job description involves the pursuit of play and enjoyment.

Well, now it's your turn. The toys I highlight later are too cool! Don't spoil the fun by worrying about how much they cost (although most are rather affordable) or how you'll ever get them into your school. Sit back and read about these playthings, let your imagination run wild, arrange a playdate with another school that already owns these trinkets, and you'll have no difficulty convincing those administrative types that these goodies are all worthy of purchase.

Chapter 5
Groovy Graphics

*W*e all can think of a few talents that we wish we had been born with. My two biggest desires are to be able to carry a tune (thank goodness first graders can't differentiate between Mariah Carey and Mrs. Robinette) and to draw. I actually get chill bumps when I'm watching a talented artist draw.

Children, on the other hand, seem to have supreme confidence in their artistic abilities.

Graphics Defined

Graphics are the still images that appear in your presentations. These images might appear in a variety of different forms: photos, line drawings, full-color pictures, scanned images, clip art, charts, or graphs.

How Can I Get These Images?

This is the really neat part: You don't have to be artistic if you want to spice up your presentations with great graphic images. A wide variety of options is available for both the artistic and nonartistic among you.

Pretend that you're Monet's great-grandchild

Even a nonartistic person like me can have fun drawing and painting on computers. The software designers have made painting and drawing software that not only accommodates the needs of those of you who are artistically inclined, but they've also included adaptations for those of us who need a little help. In addition, alternative input devices such as trackballs and digital tablets make the frustrating act of drawing with a mouse obsolete.

A difference exists between drawing and painting on the computer. Drawing programs generate very precise lines that are interpreted by the computer in the form of mathematical equations. Painting programs, on the other hand, simulate the different textures and depths created by the wide variety of artistic tools, such as paintbrushes, markers, chalks, and crayons. Paint programs record information as *bitmapped graphics,* which means that each pixel in your creation is an individual entity. (*Pixels* are tiny dots that form a grid across your computer screen.) Paint programs are a little more difficult to master, but the results look more professional and less computer-generated than those created with a draw program.

Here's a list of a few of my favorite draw - and - paint programs for school use:

- ✔ *Art Explorer* (Aldus, $42, elementary-middle school)
- ✔ *Canvas* (Deneba, $260, high school-adult)
- ✔ *Claris Draw* (Claris, $270, upper elementary school-adult)
- ✔ *Dabbler* (Fractal Design, $65, upper elementary-high school)
- ✔ *Fine Artist* (Microsoft, $48, elementary-middle school)
- ✔ *Flying Colors* (Davidson, $42, elementary-middle school)
- ✔ *Freehand* (Aldus, $390, high school-adult)
- ✔ *KidPix2* (Brøderbund, $48, elementary school)
- ✔ *SuperPaint* (Adobe, $90, high school-adult)

Remember, whenever possible you should save your creations as PICT files if you intend to use them later in your multimedia presentations. (PICT files are the most commonly recognized graphic files in the world of Mac.)

Some programs, such as *KidPix,* combine both drawing and painting capabilities that enable you to paint something that you draw.

Many of the multimedia authoring programs such as *HyperStudio, Multimedia Workshop, ClarisWorks,* and *HyperCard* have limited draw-and-paint features within them. So see if some of your needs might be met within your authoring program before investing in a draw program or paint program.

A word about image editing

High school students have tons of fun with image-editing software—altering the principal's face has never been so easy. Those who master principal alteration often go on to create amazing photos for those supermarket tabloids. *Photoshop* (Adobe, $560) is probably the most popular image-editing software on the market. The price is high, but the effects are very impressive. Image-editing programs have tools that are similar to the tools found in paint programs, except image-editing tools are used to alter an already-existing image. Image-editing programs enable you to manipulate each individual pixel in an image — they'll even work with scanned images. Another neat aspect of a program such as *Photoshop* is its ability to convert file formats — it can change an EPS file to a PICT file for you. Take a look!

Poor exposure   Corrected exposure

Transformed into a line drawing

(photo courtesy of Carl and Jeanie Siegle)

Buy them!

That's right: Just open up any of the software catalogs, and you'll find tons of companies who'd love to sell you one of their CDs full of graphics. These CDs hold thousands of images ready for you to import into your multimedia presentations.

Graphics CDs come in a variety of types including photo images, background images, maps, color clip art, and line drawings. Photos, clip art, line drawings, and maps can be used to explain or add emphasis to your subject. Background images or textures are used differently. These graphics are usually used as a canvas on which you lay your presentation. Background graphics can set your presentation apart from other presentations and add interest to a project; they also are much more exciting than a plain white screen or flat color.

A well-chosen background texture makes a big difference.

Many of these CDs come packaged with audio and video clips as well, and the prices are usually very reasonable. One of my favorite packages is the *Discovery Toolkit* (Pierian Spring Software). For around $50, you get hundreds of pictures, sound clips, and QuickTime movies.

Tip: For most of the software programs highlighted in this book, it would be best if the graphics that you purchase are saved in PICT format (see the following section about "Graphics File Formats"). All the catalogs and packages clearly state what format the images have been saved in. If you purchase graphics that are saved as EPS files, you'll first have to open them in a program such as *ClarisWorks* and then paste them into your multimedia projects.

Graphics File Formats

You will probably run across information about graphics file formats during your technology pursuits, and I'm sure that some of you would like to be familiar with the terminology.

Graphics files can be saved in a variety of forms, some of which will be difficult for you to use. Graphics can be saved as *PICT, TIFF, EPS,* or *GIF* files.

PICT files (a Macintosh object-oriented graphics file format) are the files most commonly used in education, and this is the format that you should look for when pursuing graphics for your multimedia presentations. This is also the format you should choose to save files in if you are presented with a choice.

TIFF format (tagged-image file format) was originally created by Aldus. These files take up a great deal of space and have a reputation for being difficult to transfer among programs. Many scanned images are saved as TIFF files.

EPS format (Encapsulated *PostScript*) was originally created by Adobe and relies on the PostScript language that the Mac uses to communicate with laser printers. Although these files look great when printed, they also have a reputation for causing problems.

ON THE CD

Morph madness

If you are really getting into this whole "graphic images thing," you might have fun trying your hand at some Hollywood-type special effects. *Morph* (Gryphon, $109) is a super program that allows you to create great special effects and save them as QuickTime movies or as PICT files, both of which can be used later in your multime-

dia projects. To *morph* something means to change it from one thing to another. You know, like what the Power Rangers do when they change from human to superhero. A demo version of *Morph* is included on the *Mac Multimedia For Teachers CD.*

GIF format (graphics interchange format) is most often found on America Online and other online services.

Other Input Options

Kids are always complaining that they can't get the mouse to do what they want it to do. It's very frustrating for children to plan a presentation, do all the research, and make sketches — then when it comes time to commit their efforts to digital memory (sitting down at the computer and drawing it or searching purchased CDs for that "perfect image"), things just don't seem to come together as easily as they had anticipated. In response to such frustrations, manufacturers have come up with an astounding number and variety of options for input of graphics.

Scanners

TECHNO TERMS

Scanners look and act like that copy machine you probably stand in line to use each day, and when it's your turn, you more-than-likely hold your breath and pray that it doesn't jam until the last warm copy is in you hand. However, scanners don't spit out warm sheets of paper with poor images. They give you digitized images that you can save on your hard drive or on a disk to access later and use in an amazing variety of ways.

Note: Many scanners come equipped with basic image-editing software similar to those tools provided with *Photoshop*.

Scanners come in a variety of shapes and sizes, all of which could find a snug, comfortable place on your computer table.

Flatbed

Flatbed scanners look and function much like copy machines. You place the image that you wish to scan on the glass surface and close the cover; the scanner's light source scans the image and converts it into digital information that your computer can understand. The image area of these machines varies somewhat, but most of the standard machines will accommodate legal-sized pages or larger. Flatbed scanners can run between $500 and $2,500, depending on the resolution and image area.

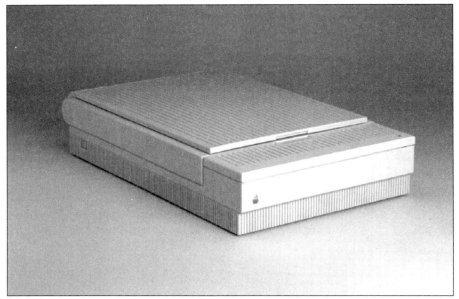

Apple flatbed scanner (photo courtesy of Apple Computer, Inc.)

Hand-held

Hand-held scanners are much less expensive than flatbed scanners, but they're also much more restrictive. With hand-held scanners, you control the light source. Controlling the light source means that a great deal of the quality in your image depends on how steady-handed you are. Size limitations also come into play here. Most of the hand-held scanners are under seven inches in width, which greatly limits their use in the school setting because most images you'll be wanting to scan are probably wider than seven inches. However, most hand-helds let you splice multiple scans together. On the positive side, hand-held scanners are substantially less expensive than any of the other styles. Hand-held scanners cost between $150 and $400 each.

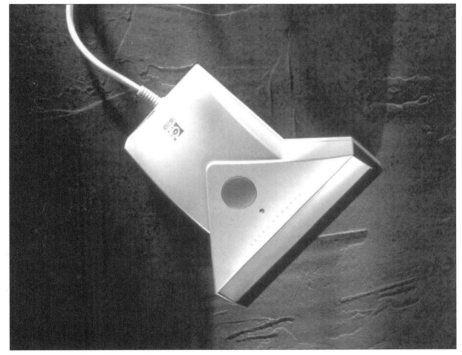

Scan Man hand-held scanner (©1995 Logitech, Inc, used by permission)

Slide scanners

Slide scanners tend to produce sharper images than flatbed and hand-held scanners do because the light passes through the image instead of reflecting off the image. These machines are easy to use and are commonplace in magazine production departments and publishing houses. These scanners start at $1,000 and go much higher.

Polaroid SprintScan 35 (photo courtesy of Polaroid Corporation)

Photo scanners

Photo scanners are relatively new on the market. They were created to scan one 3 × 5-inch picture at a time. These might be nice scanners to have for school use. They would allow students to bring in family snapshots for use within presentations. Storm makes the new EasyPhoto scanner that runs about $270. (I want one of these.)

EasyPhoto scanner (photo courtesy of Storm Software)

I'm not sure if my school could survive without our scanner. That's a gross overstatement, but we use the scanner on a daily basis when our kids are involved with multimedia projects. And the scanner is not just being used for the kids' multimedia pursuits. At the beginning of each school year, teachers scan pictures of each of their students. Then the teachers highlight a different student in their newsletter each week and include one of the scanned pictures. These images are also great for use on an "About the Author" page of a student-created presentation, book, or e-book (electronic book).

RRR (required reading on resolution)

Teachers already deal with varying rates of resolution on a daily basis: You *know* the number of words per page of homework that you can actually read at first glance. Well, in the computer world, resolution is measured by the number of *pixels* or *dots per inch (dpi)* that can be read and interpreted by equipment such as scanners, printers, and digital cameras. The higher the dpi number, the better the image.

600DPI

300DPI

Digital cameras

Digital cameras work just like regular cameras that use film. Rather than storing images on film, however, *digital cameras* store information within the camera's memory or (in some cases) on a small disk. The price of digital cameras ranges from reasonable to kinda expensive to really expensive, and the level of quality seems to be in direct correlation to the cost.

Connectix QuickCam

There's no excuse for not buying this little camera. It shoots both still pictures (320 × 240 pixels, 4-bit grayscale) and graphics. Best of all, it'll only set you back $99. (*Grayscale* refers to an image that is composed solely of shades of gray. The bit number refers to the number of shades.

This camera is very easy to use. (I didn't even have to read the directions.) A QuickFrame feature even allows you to save pictures to your computer's desktop — just like you'd have a framed photo on your desk at school.

Unlike all the other cameras, the QuickCam has to be hooked up to your computer (via the printer or modem port) in order to work. Another point against it might be that the pictures are only in black and white (although I've been told that a color version is just around the corner).

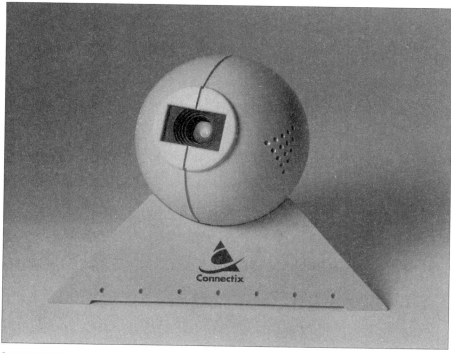

Connectix QuickCam (photo courtesy of Connectix Corporation)

Apple QuickTake 150

This camera is incredibly easy to use. The cost is in the medium range, and the photos produced are actually pretty good. It's portable. It shoots 32 average-quality (or 16 high-quality) photos before you have to download them into the computer. Resolution on all images is 640 × 480 pixels. To download pictures, you simply connect the camera to your computer with one cable. The cost (about $650) makes the QuickTake an easy purchase to convince PTA officers or school administrators to consider. Most schools in my area try to buy two or three QuickTakes because they are so popular.

Here are some hints for using the Apple QuickTake 150:

- ✔ If you go on a trip and will need to take more than 32 images (the maximum before downloading to your computer), take along a laptop and download the images to the laptop (but first make sure that you've loaded your QuickTake software on the laptop). By taking this hint, you'll be able to continue shooting throughout the trip.

- ✔ You'll want to buy the little extras that go along with the QuickTake: a battery booster pack (for those long trips) and a travel case. (Carrying your QuickTake around in the box it came in just isn't cool.)

- ✔ *Apple PhotoFlash 2.0* software makes it easy to catalog the images obtained by the QuickTake 150.

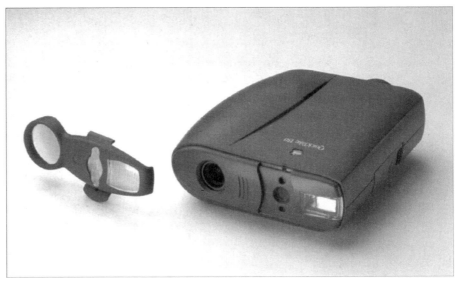

Apple QuickTake 150 (photo courtesy of Apple Computer, Inc.)

Kodak DC 40

This camera has just hit the stores and has received wonderful reviews. I've been told that it's comparable to the Canon Xap (see the next section), but the price of the DC 40 is much more reasonable — around $900.

Kodak helped develop the Apple QuickTake camera and seems to have taken that technology one step further with the introduction of the Kodak DC 40. The DC 40's resolution is much higher than that of the QuickTake (756×504 pixels), and the DC 40 can store up to 48 images before downloading to your computer. Other advantages include the capability to change lenses and adjust exposure. I look forward to seeing this camera in more schools (including mine) very soon.

Kodak Digital Camera 40 (photo courtesy of Eastman Kodak Co.)

Canon Xap

Canon's camera provides the highest quality images. It's also the most expensive. The Xap (pronounced *zap*) takes color photos that are stored on a special disk provided by Canon. Many folks swear by this camera. It also comes with super image-editing capabilities. Just as you can with the Kodak DC 40, you can adjust the exposure and use a variety of lenses with the Xap. This camera will set you back about $1,500; but if you are really into digital imaging, it's worth it.

Canon RC-360 still video camera (photo courtesy of Canon U.S.A., INC.)

Digitizer tablets

Digitizer tablets come in a variety of sizes and look like thick sheets of plastic, only guess what? These thick sheets of plastic are loaded with tiny little sensors that track the movements of a pen or stylus as it moves across the tablet. Most of the newer tablets can also register the amount of pressure coming from the pen, which allows more true artistic use. The tablets are even sensitive enough to enable students (or teachers) to trace over a sheet of paper. What a dream: No more complaints about not being able to draw with a mouse. These tablets work great with drawing and painting programs. As a matter of fact, many of the tablets now come bundled with painting and drawing software. I used one of these cool inventions for the first time while writing this book. I'm truly shocked that more schools haven't discovered how easy to use and accommodating these tablets can be. Special education students and younger students who have trouble with a mouse would love the ease-of-use provided by these little jewels.

CalComp Drawing Slate II (photo courtesy of CalComp)

Trackballs

Some of my artist friends can't believe that I still use a mouse. They use a trackball, which gives them more control over their drawing. Many parents also start their children off using a trackball because mouse manipulation is difficult for children (and even some adults) to master.

A *trackball* works like a mouse that's been turned upside down. You simply roll your hand over the ball. You click by pressing down on buttons located on either side of the ball. Microsoft even makes a kid's version of the trackball that's bigger and even easier to handle.

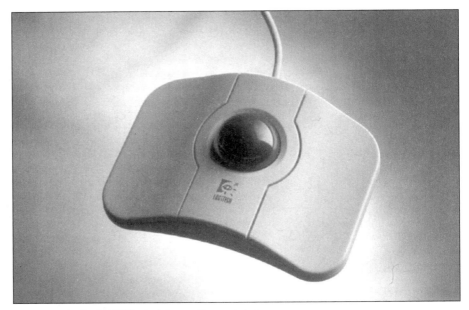

Logitech First Trackball (©1995 Logitech, Inc,. used by permission)

Photo CDs

I've mentioned *photo CDs* in the book already; however, I really think more teachers should be taking advantage of this technology. It's simple: You take pictures with your 35mm camera, ask your local processor to have the pictures developed and then stored on a Kodak Photo CD, and wait about a week. The first time you have pictures processed this way, the cost will be about $35 because you'll also be paying for the actual CD itself; but you can add onto this CD the next time you have photos developed, and the cost will be much less. (Each CD holds about 100 pictures.)

The images are stored on your CD in a variety of different resolution levels from thumbnail-sized to 3072×2048 pixels. Kodak's *SlideShow Viewer* software makes it easy to view your masterpieces, and many of the multimedia composition programs you'll be using will enable you simply to cut or copy and paste the images into your presentations.

The poor man's substitute for a digital camera

If you have an AV Mac and a video camera, you have digital photo capabilities within your reach! Simply hook your video camera up to the Video In jack on the back of your AV Mac. Then open the Video Monitor file (or Apple Video Player, depending on your Mac model) on your hard drive. The next thing you'll see on your monitor is a screen showing what you're seeing through your camera's lens. You can control the brightness with the slider bar on the bottom of the screen. When you like what you see, hold down the ⌘-C combination. You'll hear a click that sounds like a camera taking a picture. The pictures you take will be saved on your desktop as PICT 1, PICT 2, and so forth.

Note: If you purchase an AV card, the software that comes with your card has these capabilities as well.

Okay, now that you've captured the sights, let's add the sound and movement. Keep reading!

The 5th Wave

By Rich Tennant

"WELL! IT LOOKS LIKE SOMEONE FOUND THE 'LION'S ROAR' ON THE SOUND CONTROL PANEL!"

Chapter 6
Sound Advice

In This Chapter

▶ Why a teacher should bring more sound into the classroom

▶ Types of sounds (none of which involve putting your hand under your arm)

▶ Getting the sounds into your computer

▶ School realities

▶ Extra info you can skip if you want to

*T*wo types of people live in this world: those who must have some type of noise in order to function and those who crave silence. I fall into the quiet category; while I'm outside working in the yard or sitting on the beach, I love to hear only the sounds of nature. My husband, on the other hand, needs background noise. He likes to have a radio playing and can't stand it when the house is totally silent (which is a rare occurrence when you have two toddlers).

Kids have come to expect background noises and sound effects. Try this experiment: Close your eyes and just listen the next time your child is watching cartoons or playing a video game. The number and intensity of the sound effects will amaze you. As a matter of fact, I would venture to say that the sound effects are almost as important as the visual images in a media presentation.

Why Do I Need Sound?

You say your classroom is already noisy enough? Well I say why not take advantage of the noisemaking capabilities of your students and create productive noises (sounds) that can be used to enhance your multimedia productions.

There are three basic uses for sound within a multimedia project: sound effects, narration, and background music.

Sound effects

Why not start out with the one that will most interest your students. Go ahead and see how excited they get when you tell them that you need their help in adding sound effects to the World War II presentation. Or challenge them to come up with the best bubbling-brook sound for a Gold Rush production.

Sound effects production is big business in Hollywood. The people behind some of the most realistic sound effects are very creative. Adding good sound effects increases the Wow Factor. You know what I mean: The Wow Factor occurs when people are watching your production and you hear them exclaim "Wow! This is incredible!" or "I can't believe how talented these kids are!"

Narration

Good narration is sometimes the key to understanding a multimedia production. And while reading text may not seem nearly as exciting as creating the sounds for a battle scene, the narrator's job is very important.

Narration enables students to communicate directly with the intended audience. What is being said is important; it needs to be clear, concise, and correct. I often have students wait and write the narration after the project is put together. That way I ensure that it all flows together nicely and that what is being said (narration) matches the visual images in the presentation.

Background music

Setting the mood for your production is important. You wouldn't want to play an upbeat tune while showing soldiers leaving a Civil War battlefield, and '70s disco music seems out of place while you are watching an informative production about Ancient Greece.

Musical choices should match the intended audience and subject matter. Have your students research the musical style of the time period you are studying. Ask questions about your intended audience: "Do you think the city council will pay attention to your new mall proposal if you have Guns and Roses playing in the background?"

Music also makes the less-interactive screens (title page, credits, written text) more enjoyable.

Getting the Sound into Your Computer

Before you can put these great sounds into your presentations, the sounds have to get into your computer. Storing sounds in your computer involves converting the sounds into a digital format.

As I've said before, the Mac is a multimedia machine. All of the new Macs (and most of the older models) come equipped with basic multimedia components including Audio In. Some Macs also come with a microphone, which allows you to record sounds directly into your computer.

To record a sound that you wish to use in a multimedia production, you must first open the Sound control panel. You'll find this file in your System folder in the Control Panels folder. Double click the Sound icon to view the Sound control panel.

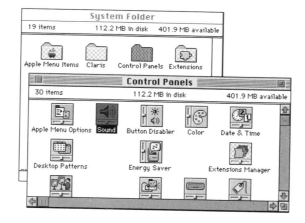

Depending upon your System software, the control panels will look like the following:

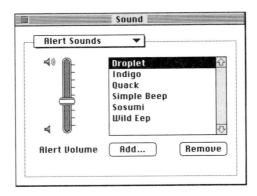

Recording a sound

The Alert Sounds button has an arrow pointing down, which means that it has a pull-down menu containing other choices. Pull this menu down and choose Input Source.

Few choices exist when it comes to Macintosh microphones. There's the internal microphone that's built into some Macs and the external microphone that may look either like a little round pill case (in older Macs) or like a tea bag (in newer Macs).

For now, the external microphone will work just fine; and in addition, external microphones usually come as part of your school's computer purchase.

To add a sound, simply click the Add button on the Sound control panel, and a screen appears that looks like the controls of a tape recorder.

The little speaker icon will show you the sound input level. Before clicking Record, speak into the microphone. If you see little lines coming out of the speaker icon, sound is going into your computer. If you don't see these lines, check to be sure that the microphone is inserted in the port or check and make sure that you've chosen the correct input source.

Now simply click the Record button to record your sound. After you've finished recording, click Stop. Play back the sound and see whether you did a good job. If not, try recording again. Don't click Save until you're happy with your recording. You'll be prompted to give your sound a name. Then click OK.

The sound is now saved as a System Sound and can be used in other programs. To use it in other programs, simply drag the saved sound from the System file into the Sounds folder of whatever program you want to use.

Note: Most of the multimedia production programs I've described in the book enable you to add a sound during the production's creation process. However, by entering a sound in the System folder, you'll have access to that sound in every program you may use. This method keeps you from having to re-record a sound effect each time you want to use it in a different production.

You can also enter sound directly from another source such as a tape recorder, mixer, CD-ROM drive, or VCR. All you need is a cable that has a double phono plug on the source end and a $1/8$-inch stereo miniplug for the Mac's microphone jack on the other end.

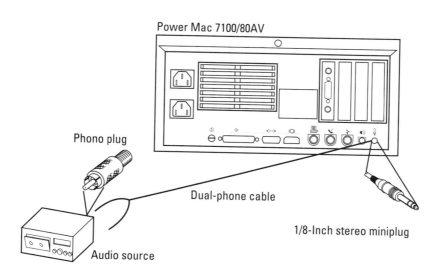

Power Mac 7100/80AV

Phono plug

Dual-phone cable

1/8-Inch stereo miniplug

Audio source

Software and CD-ROM clips

Software and CD-ROM products are available that contain royalty-free sound clips for use in multimedia projects. A couple of my favorites are *Kaboom!* (Nova Development, $49.95) and *PictSounds* (Monarch Software, $51.95).

Audio CDs

They sound so good!

If you want to add your favorite Garth Brooks tune to your presentation, you'll run into a few problems. This tune is copyrighted material. You'll need to obtain permission for use if you plan on showing your presentation anywhere outside your classroom.

Listening to Garth while you grade papers, on the other hand, is very legal and easy to do — provided you have a CD-ROM drive connected to your computer.

Put the CD in your drive. After its icon appears, go to the Apple Menu and choose Apple CD Audio Player or CD Remote. (If you don't see these files in your Apple Menu, look in the Extensions folder.)

Next, you'll see a set of controls that looks just like those on your CD player. Go ahead and try them. (If the CD-ROM player is external, you need to connect a set of powered speakers for this to work.)

MIDI

MIDI (musical instrument digital interface) enables you to use an electronic keyboard, drum machine, or mixer (you have to use a MIDI interface costing about $70) to record your own music. Your creations can then be played back using MIDI equipment (or through a sound digitizer), recorded as digital audio, and used in your productions.

Note: The Mac Music & Sound Forum (keyword **MMS**) on America Online is full of MIDI information, discussions, and resources.

Mommy's gentle reminder

Another cool thing you can do while visiting the Sound control panel is change your alert sound. That's the sound your computer makes when you don't follow directions. You can choose any of your saved sounds to become your alert sound. When my daughter was two years old, she would say "I don't fink so Mommy" when I'd ask her certain questions. (*Fink* was her precious two-year-old's way of saying *think*.)

I recorded her saying this phrase and then chose it as my alert sound by highlighting it on the Sound control panel.

Now, whenever I do something wrong, I hear her sweet voice, and my error doesn't seem so awful!

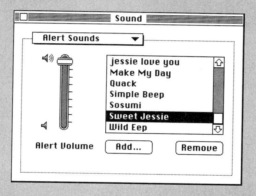

Speakers

Your Mac doesn't come with the best set of speakers. Actually, the sounds you are recording probably sound better than you think they do. The Mac records sound at a good quality — but without a good set of speakers, you don't know how good it really is.

One option that you have is to use your stereo's speakers. That's right. Scoot on down to your local Radio Shack and get yourself a cable that has a pair of male RCA plugs on one end and a male miniplug on the other. Put the miniplug in your Mac's speaker jack and plug the RCA plugs into the back of your stereo's Aux (or Tape) inputs.

The easier (yet more expensive) option is to purchase a set of powered computer speakers. Such speakers range in price and quality, but even the cheapest speakers seem better than the Mac's capabilities.

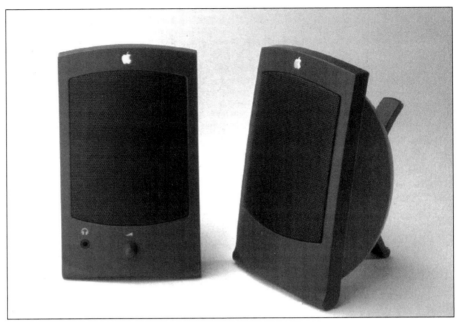

Apple Powered Speakers II (photo courtesy of Apple Computer, Inc.)

School Realities

No, I'm not talking about things like the lack of phones available for you to use when you need to make a personal call — although that *is* a school reality. I'm talking about the limitations of time and space.

Space

One of the most frustrating aspects of adding sound to your presentations will be finding a good space to record. Classrooms, by nature, have horrible acoustics, not to mention 25 or more precious (yet noisy) children. I've found closets or administrators' offices to be a better choice. (Carpet on the floor would be an added bonus.)

Time

I prefer to add sound to my productions toward the end of the process. Waiting until the production is nearly finished before adding sound helps to ensure the overall continuity of the product. Time constraints may prevent this luxury, so plan ahead and make the best use of your time.

It also helps things go more quickly if you can work with one or two students at a time while recording. Nothing is quite as frustrating as recording in a classroom full of students and having one child giggle at the end of an otherwise perfect take.

Stuff You May Not Care About

The next few tidbits may not make sense or sound too exciting to you right now. However, as you become a true multimedia mogul, they may all become relevant and make more sense.

Sound-editing software

Sound-editing software programs help you do things like copy, cut, and paste sounds, decide how long sounds play, and eliminate portions of sound from a sound clip. Manipulating the sounds you record can be loads of fun. It can also become a time-consuming process. By using sound-editing software, you can also do some audio mixing. Audio mixing involves adding sound enhancements to an already-existing sound, such as the sound enhancement of your voice over already-recorded music.

Sampling rate

The *sampling rate* refers to how much audio information is recorded by the computer in one second. This ratio has a direct relationship to the quality of sound. This ratio is measured in kilohertz (kHz). The higher the kilohertz, the more superb the sound quality.

Sound file size

So you know that you want high-quality sound, right? Well, I'm sorry to have to break it to you, but the higher the sound quality, the more hard-disk space you'll need. A simple 30-second sound sample at 11 kHz takes up 330K of space . . . and that's not very high-quality sound. Go up to 22 kHz for the same amount of time, and you're looking at 660K of space. That's over half a meg! And that's only 30 seconds of time!

Sound secrets

Most multimedia presentation programs have commands that enable you to decrease or increase the sampling rate of your recordings. Using these commands enables you to obtain a higher quality of sound without the use of sound-editing software.

In *KidPix Studio* you simply hold down the ⌘ key while you click the microphone icon.

Doing so decreases your recording time from 32 seconds to 16 seconds and increases the quality of your recording substantially.

HyperStudio has a similar secret. For better sound, hold down the ⌘ key while you record. For the best sound, hold down the option key while you record.

Chapter 7
Victory over Video

· ·

In This Chapter

▶ What's the big deal?

▶ Getting the video in your computer

▶ QuickTime queries

▶ Laser disc laments

▶ Apple does animation

· ·

I'll admit it . . . I'm more comfortable with my computer than I am with my VCR. But then again, I'm the same teacher who used to break into a cold sweat when I wanted to show those 16mm films — I just knew that the machine would jam or that the return reel wouldn't catch and the entire film would wind up in a snake-like pile on the floor.

The Age of Video

We've come a long way, baby! Videotapes are easy to use and oh-so-accessible. And video cameras are tons of fun. Most schools are now equipped with a good supply of videotapes (that, of course, correlate with the curriculum), an army of VCRs, and (hopefully) a video camera or two.

Whole books have been written on the artful use of the video camera, and I hope that you've used a video camera at least once or twice with your students. If you do nothing else, get a blank tape for the beginning of each school year and record classroom highlights as they occur. At the end of the year, you'll have a retrospective that the kids will enjoy watching.

I know: You thought this book was about computers. Well, guess what? Now you can show video footage on your Mac. That's right; you can even include video as a part of a multimedia presentation.

What makes it all possible

Well, you really shouldn't be able to have movies playing on your Mac — but then again, who would have ever thought you'd even have a Mac? You see, video signals are analog, but your computer can only read digital information. In addition, in order for your monitor to be able to display images in the way and at the size they're seen on TV, the computer would have to be able to process information at the breakneck rate of 30 frames per second.

Let's take a look at the ways those clever techno-heads at Apple overcame these two obstacles.

AV cards and AV Macs

An *AV card* (audiovisual card) changes those nasty little analog signals into digital or binary information that your Mac can understand. AV cards can be purchased separately for about $500 each and can be installed in your Mac; or you can purchase a higher-end Mac with an AV card already installed. You'll know a higher-end Mac is an AV Mac because it'll have the letters AV after the name — 6100 AV or Quadra 840 AV, for example. (I want one of these *really* bad. Until then, I'll have to be happy with having access to one at school.)

It's good to have at least one AV Mac in your school. After you've gotten video footage into your computer, not only can you play the video and include it in other programs, but you can also manipulate the images by applying filters, adding color, taking out portions, adding transitions, and performing a variety of other options. Another neat thing you can do with an AV Mac is transfer all of your cool manipulations and multimedia presentations back into analog form on a VHS tape. I love this capability because it enables me to make videotapes of the kids' presentations and then show the videotapes on classroom VCRs or via our closed-circuit television system.

QuickTime technology

QuickTime isn't a program that you use with your Mac. QuickTime is an extension that's part of System 7 and higher (but you can use QuickTime on pre-System 7 machines, also). QuickTime enables your Mac to combine audio, video, and animation into a single QuickTime file. Then all kinds of cool stuff is possible! Those QuickTime files can be played through the QuickTime player component that comes with most Macs. The neat thing about QuickTime is that any QuickTime file can be shuffled from program to program just as if it were a graphics file; and because QuickTime is an extension, it doesn't require any particular software program in order to function. QuickTime movies aren't difficult to run either. The control strip at the bottom of the picture window allows a simple click to start the magic.

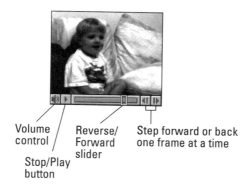

Volume control / Stop/Play button / Reverse/Forward slider / Step forward or back one frame at a time

QuickTime movies can add a dramatic effect to your multimedia presentations. As far as that goes, QuickTime movies can add pizzazz to something as simple as a letter to Grandma.

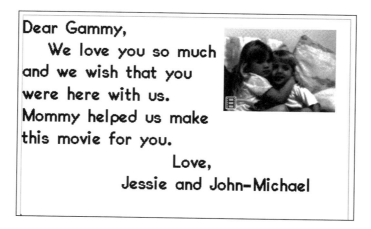

Dear Gammy,
    We love you so much and we wish that you were here with us. Mommy helped us make this movie for you.
                Love,
        Jessie and John-Michael

Getting those movies into your productions is easy. You have two choices: shoot them yourself or buy them.

Shoot it yourself

If you don't have an AV Mac, you'll have to purchase an AV card. The most popular AV cards are the Apple AV card, VideoSpigot, and Movie Movie. (Check with your retailer to make sure that your Mac has the proper NuBus or PDS slots to accommodate the card you intend to purchase.) You also need to make sure that you are running System 7 and have at least 5MB of RAM installed.

Installation of an AV card is a simple process. The cards always come with a great set of directions (pictures, too). The card simply slides into an open slot inside your Mac, and your audio and video ports pop out a slot in the back of your Mac. Then you simply load the provided software so that your Mac knows you've added another capability, and you're set.

Plug your TV, VCR, or camcorder into the AV card; or with an AV Mac, plug your video source into the Video In jack on the back of the Mac. AV cards all come with their own recording software. If you have an AV Mac, the recording software that came with your Mac is called *Apple Video Player*. Open this program or the one that came with your AV card (don't worry; they're all pretty much the same) and you'll see a very easy-to-understand window with such controls as Record, Stop, and Play.

Click the Record button when you're ready, and you'll create your own QuickTime movie. The program will prompt you to name the movie and save it. Now it's ready to be used in any of your multimedia or word processing creations.

Buy it

Just as you can buy clip art and photographs for your own use, you can buy QuickTime movies that are ready to be used in your productions. Often, you'll find movies grouped with other graphics on a CD; additional movies might be found in encyclopedias or other reference CDs. See Chapter 16 for a great list of resources for multimedia production.

If you buy QuickTime movies on a CD (or maybe buy a combination of clip art, photos, and QuickTime movies), the contents of such CDs (you know, the pictures, sounds, and movies) are usually royalty free — there are no legal ramifications if you choose to use them in your productions. However, movies that are on reference CDs may have royalty or copyright restrictions. Read the fine print that comes with your CD and become familiar with the copyright limitations. Your media specialist (or librarian) can provide you with information on copyright law.

Quintessential QuickTime

I recently saw the most amazing QuickTime movie. Some students were researching World War II. In the *Time Almanac Reference Edition* CD, they found a movie showing Adolph Hitler who was giving a speech. I was amazed! Of course he was speaking in German, but his anger and contempt came through loud and clear.

As a child, I had read about and had been told about what a horrible, misguided man Hitler was. But to see him in action in this movie made everything my teachers had told me about this madman seem so real. Viewing the movie had a profound effect on the kids as well. That's only one example of the advantages today's students have. Rather than imagining (based on what we teachers so artfully and engagingly tell them), they can view actual film footage.

Limitation lament

QuickTime technology isn't perfect — yet. I know that, very soon, the people at Apple will have improved the computers and tweaked the QuickTime extension to the point of perfection. Until then, there are two major limitations: size of the movie and amount of memory involved.

Itsy-bitsy movies

One of the reasons QuickTime is even able to happen on your computer is because of the reduced playback-window size. If you increase the screen size as you record the movie or when you play the movie back, it will become jerky and distorted. The smaller the screen, the smoother the playback.

The larger screen becomes distorted.

 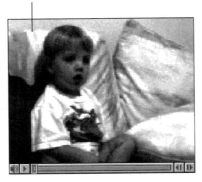

Memory monster

QuickTime movies take up major amounts of memory. I'm talking about a rate of around 30MB or so of hard drive space (depending on the screen size) for each four minutes of video shot. (I know — isn't that wild?)

I once had to dump just about everything off of my hard drive just to record and save a one-minute-long QuickTime movie. This is where it helps to have a large hard drive or an external hard drive.

Other "Video-Like" Stuff

I know that the word *stuff* is a horrible word. If my students use that word, I ask them to describe the stuff they are talking about. So that's just what I'm going to do: describe other video-like stuff, such as laser disc clips and animation, that is both visually fun and informative.

Laser discs

Laser discs are sometimes referred to as video discs. They're about 12 inches in diameter and, like CDs, hold tons-of-info. In order to play a laser disc, you'll need a laser disc player, which costs about $1,000 or less. You can purchase the players and discs from any of the mail-order houses mentioned in Chapter 20. The coolest thing about laser discs is that they are all *encoded,* which means that each segment (and sometimes each frame) has a separate barcode.

With a key of listings and actual barcodes for each listing provided in the teacher's guide, you can set up a presentation that's based on information you need for a lesson or multimedia project and skip over the stuff that's not applicable to your teaching situation. A barcode reader can be purchased from any hardware dealer at a cost of between $150 and $250. It helps to have a barcode reader when you're setting up a presentation; otherwise you'll spend a great deal of time punching in the barcode numbers by hand.

A laser disc player can be hooked up to your television (to view) and hooked up to your computer (to control) via your modem port.

Be sure that you plan before using a laser disc program. Laser discs contain lots of information, and the whole purpose behind using them for classroom instruction (or including portions of them in presentations) is that you can access specific information on them. Don't waste valuable classroom time scanning through each segment.

Many of the multimedia presentation software titles, such as *HyperStudio*, enable you to import portions of laser disc media. When you import such portions, the laser disc information is stored as a QuickTime movie.

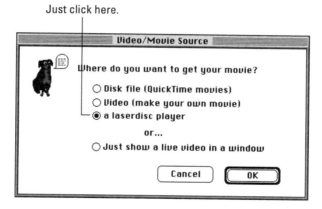

Care for laser discs in the same way that you care for CDs. In general, laser discs are much more durable than CDs and software disks.

There aren't nearly as many laser disc programs on the market as there are software or CD programs, and laser discs cost a bit more (between $50 and $400 a title). Most laser disc programs are very specific, however, and delve much more deeply into their subject matter than their CD or software counterparts. And with the use of the barcode reader, lessons can be customized with laser disc chips that enhance the content. Here are a few of my favorite laser disc titles:

✔ *Ancient Egypt* (Voyager, $124.95)

✔ *Dinosaur!* (Lumivision, $69.95)

✔ *The Dream Is Alive* (Lumivision, $39.95)

- *__The Great Ocean Rescue__* (Voyager, $349.95)
- *__National Gallery of Art__* (Voyager, $94.95)
- *__Titanic__* (Lumivision, $79.95)
- *__Tropical Rainforest__* (Lumivision, $79.95)
- *__Visual Almanac__* (Voyager, $129.95)
- *__A World Alive__* (Voyager, $ 49.95)

Animation

Animation has really come to the forefront with computers. Disney and many other Hollywood studios are now using computer-generated animation instead of always drawing their images on film cels by hand. Software companies are starting to realize that kids can do this type of artwork, and animation capabilities are now included as part of most of the multimedia presentation software packages.

Claris has a program, *Amazing Animation*, that is devoted to animated images and multimedia presentation. This program is too cool! Not only can you create animated screens, but the program has three different levels of expertise that enable a teacher to best meet each student's individual level of expertise. After kids start using this program, it's hard to stop them.

HyperStudio, *KidPix2*, and *KidPix Studio* also have built-in animation features that make it easy to include many other forms of media along with animated segments. All of these programs make it very easy to incorporate animation into your presentation — just follow the directions as they appear on your screen or (heaven forbid) read the manual.

Remember, animation doesn't have to be interpreted as a cartoon character with a silly voice. My students have used animation to show a route some explorers took, to show the sun's place in the sky at different times of the day, and to show the life cycle of the butterfly.

Okay, you've read about all the multimedia components. Now it's time to get busy. Read Part III to get the lowdown on how to use the multimedia production software, pick a project, and go for it!

Part III
Just Do It!

"Of course graphics are important to your project, Eddy, but I think it would've been better to scan a <u>picture</u> of your worm collection."

In this part . . .

You've read about all the neat "toys" you can use with your computer. You believe in the concepts behind multimedia in the school. You've even purchased a few CDs of media clips. So let's get on with it already!

In this part you'll learn the basics involved with creating multimedia presentations using *ClarisWorks, KidPix Studio,* and *HyperStudio.* You'll also discover a wealth of ideas for projects that integrate curriculum and technology. And finally, I'll lay out a plan of action for you to help get things going.

Chapter 8

Simple Multimedia Stuff You Can Do with *ClarisWorks*

In This Chapter

▶ Inserting a QuickTime movie into a word processing document

▶ Creating a *ClarisWorks* slide show

And you thought *ClarisWorks* was just for creating documents you can print. In my first book, *Macs For Teachers* (IDG Books Worldwide, 1995), I compared *ClarisWorks* to a loaded spud because *ClarisWorks* is like a baked potato with *all* the toppings. In one neat package, *ClarisWorks* gives you word processing, spreadsheets, data bases, painting, drawing, and communications. And now I've got two additional toppings to tell you about: One is the capability to insert movies into just about any document; the other is slide show presentations that are as simple to create as word processing documents are.

Hey, There's a Movie in This Report!

If your computer has the QuickTime extension (see Chapter 7), you can do some really cool stuff with a simple word processing document.

You may have seen the Apple television commercial that was broadcast frequently in the late summer of 1994. It featured a young boy working on a report about his vacation. The boy was at a Mac with his dad, and they were viewing the written report that was visible on their Mac's screen. The next part was what impressed me: They pulled up video footage of their vacation and inserted it into the report. Before the commercial was finished, this kid had not only created a report that told about his summer vacation in words, but he had also incorporated video footage into his report that showed what he did on his vacation *as a movie!* The commercial didn't tell you that the boy was using an AV model, and I thought that my school would never be able to afford a Mac that could perform such incredible feats.

I was wrong. Before you know it, all schools will have access to amazing machines such as these. But for now, you, too, can work some minor miracles of your own.

If you have an AV Mac or a computer with an AV card, I encourage you to create your own QuickTime movies (see Chapter 7) for this next activity. If you don't have a Mac with AV capabilities, you can still participate — just go out and buy yourself a CD or two (see Chapter 16) and use the ready-made QuickTime clips.

Getting your movie on the page

First, I'd like you to create a letter in the Word Processing mode of *ClarisWorks*. (If you're not familiar with word processing, you might want to take a look at Chapter 7 in *Macs For Teachers,* IDG Books Worldwide, 1995.)

1. At the bottom of your screen, click the Tool panel to make it appear.

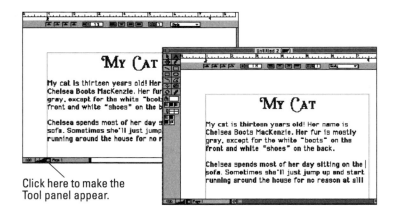

Click here to make the
Tool panel appear.

2. Click the arrow tool.

3. From the File menu, choose Insert.

4. Locate and highlight the QuickTime movie you want to insert and click the Insert button.

The movie should now appear on your screen.

5. While the handles are on the movie, you are free to move it (by dragging) to any location. Now click anywhere on your word processing document, and your handles will disappear. (If handles do not appear on your movie, you didn't follow Step 2. Press Delete and try again.)

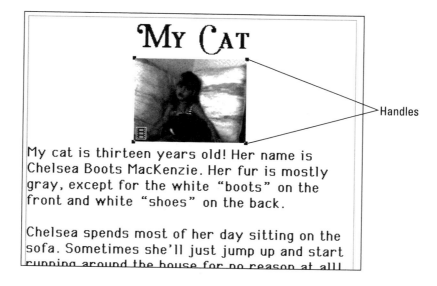

Setting options

Now set some options.

1. After you've got the movie where you want it on your document, click once on the movie itself, and handles should appear.

2. After the movie gets its handles, go to the Options menu and choose Movie Info.

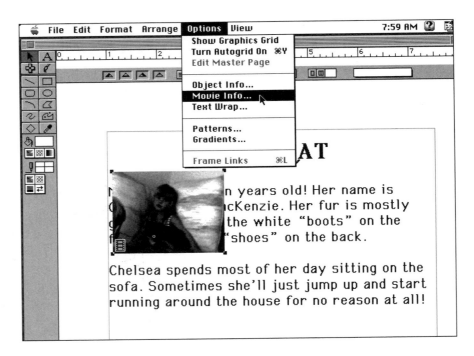

This choice gives you a dialog box that lets you control both the speed of your playback (leave this setting at 1 if your movie has sound) and whether you want the movie to *loop* (play over and over again).

Now you're ready to go.

Where's my control bar?

When the movie first appears on your screen, you may not see the traditional QuickTime control bar. Instead, you may see a small badge that looks like a strip of film in the bottom, left-hand corner.

1. Click the badge. After you click this badge, the movie control bar should appear. If the bar doesn't appear, its absence means that you inserted the movie as in-line text (that is, you didn't choose the arrow tool before inserting).

2. Delete your movie by clicking once on the movie to get handles and then pressing the Delete key. Then start again.

Click the badge to make the
movie control bar appear.

A few notes

Note 1: If you create a report like the one in this example, you'd probably have to send it through a modem (using any e-mail package or via America Online as an attached file) to the intended receiver. Any document with a QuickTime movie would probably not fit on a standard floppy disk. Also note that the person receiving the file would have to have *ClarisWorks* (with QuickTime) in order to open the file.

Note 2: You say that movie is just too darn small for your tastes? Well, resizing is an option. While the handles are on your movie, you may pull or stretch it to any size that pleases you. You must note, however, that the larger you make the image, the more clarity you lose; and depending on which Mac you have, you may even have some problems with playback (the playback may be jerky).

Note 3: Although this example used the Word Processing mode of *ClarisWorks*, you can insert QuickTime movies into draw documents, into spreadsheet documents, and into the layout portion of a database.

Note 4: If you are adding a movie to an existing word processing document and you don't have an open space to insert a little movie, you can always choose Text Wrap from the Options menu. This option will work your text around the movie.

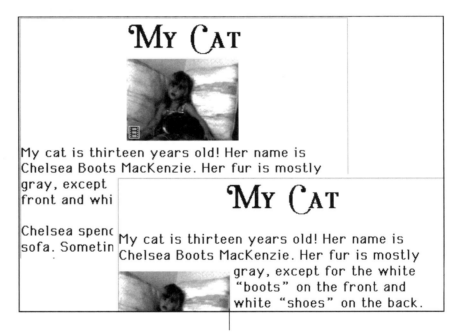

Text wraps around the movie.

Note 5: Don't be intimidated! With *ClarisWorks,* inserting movies is fun stuff.

ClarisWorks Slide Shows

The slide show function in *ClarisWorks* isn't as flashy as the one in *KidPix Studio,* but hey, I think that *ClarisWorks* has already done plenty to earn its place in the Software Hall of Fame.

Creating a slide show in *ClarisWorks* is fairly simple. Don't worry. I'm going to start you out slowly with a simple two-slide presentation. Are you ready?

1. From the New Document dialog box, choose Word Processing.

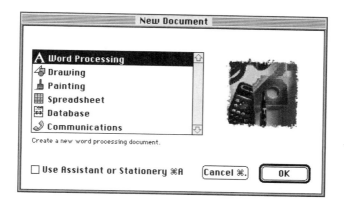

2. From the File menu, choose Page Setup. Under Orientation, choose the landscape (horizontal) image and click OK.

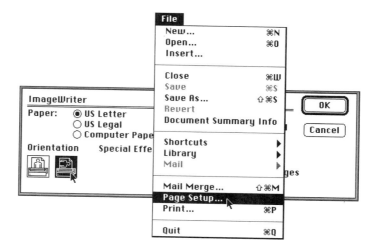

3. From the Format menu, choose Document.

4. Make the following change to this dialog box: Set all the margins to 0. Click OK.

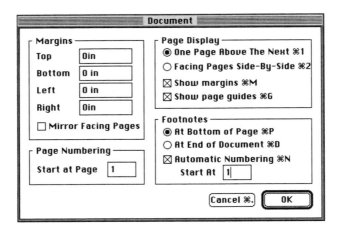

5. In the bottom-left corner of the screen, you should see the number 100. Click (and hold) this number, and a set of percentages should appear. Drag up to 50% and let go. (Reducing the size makes it easier to see your entire slide on the screen.)

Now you're ready to create your slides. Don't worry about a background color. You'll choose that later.

6. After you finish your first slide (the first page of your word processing document), choose Insert Page Break from the Format menu.

Go on and create both of your slides — add some text, maybe a graphic or two, even a QuickTime movie (follow the directions found in the first section of this chapter).

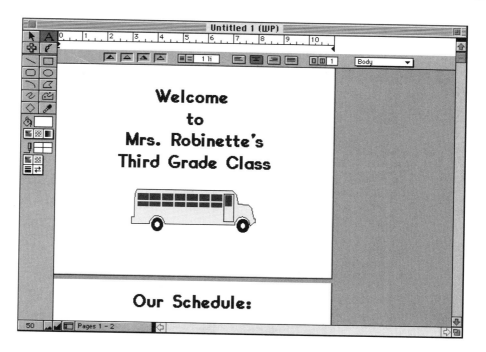

7. Now, everyone to a seat. We're about to have a show! Go to the View menu and choose Slide Show.

We now see the ever-confusing Slide Show dialog box. You can play around with these choices later.

8. For now, choose Fit to screen and Center under Slide Options and click inside the Background box to reveal your color choices.

9. Choose Fade and type in the number of seconds you want to wait before displaying the next slide.

   If you added a QuickTime movie to any of your slides, choose Auto play.

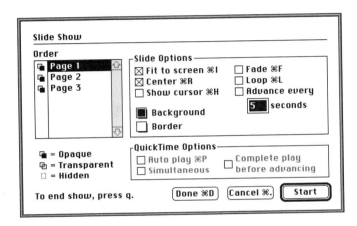

10. Click Done to save the settings.

    This action will take you back to the slides. To view your show, choose Slide Show from the View menu again and click Start. (If you want to avoid returning to this dialog box each time you make this choice, hold down the Option key when you choose Slide Show from the View menu, and your slide show should start right away.) Your first slide should appear.

    You can wait for the slide to change automatically or simply click the mouse to move forward through the slide sequence. When you want to quit, simply press Q on your keyboard.

Cheating!

Just as you eventually had to memorize those multiplication tables and throw away the cheat sheet, I feel that it's important for you to learn to create a slide show on your own. However, if you're short on time (what teacher isn't) and you're using either Version 3.0 or Version 4.0 of *ClarisWorks*, there's a cheat sheet waiting for you that doesn't involve writing on your palm with a messy ballpoint pen.

After you open *ClarisWorks* (or choose New from the File menu while you're using *ClarisWorks*), click Use Assistant or Stationery; you are presented with a screen that looks something like the following:

Scroll down the list of available assistants until you see Presentation and then double-click to open. What follows is a handholding lesson that allows you to create a really neat presentation. The catch is that Claris has done it all for you — this lesson isn't a tutorial where you are learning each step involved. It's more of a fill-in-the-blank worksheet. And, like any good teacher, I frown upon cheating. I won't call your mother this time, but I expect you to learn how to do this task on your own, eventually.

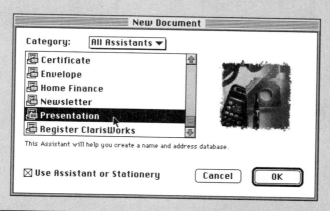

Well, I believe that this chapter added another topping or two to that loaded spud of a program, *ClarisWorks*. I hope that you have fun utilizing every facet of this great piece of software.

The 5th Wave — By Rich Tennant

"I found these two in the multimedia lab morphing faculty members into farm animals."

Chapter 9
An Overview of *KidPix Studio*

In This Chapter

▶ *KidPix Studio* capabilities

▶ Satisfying slide shows

● ●

KidPix Studio is a great program to use as an introduction to multimedia when you're working with younger students (kindergarten through third grade). Many of you may already be familiar with its predecessor, *KidPix,* which is considered by most people in the computer industry to be the best children's software program ever created.

KidPix Studio takes the familiar working environment of *KidPix* and adds tons of specialized features that fall perfectly into the category of multimedia. In this chapter, I'll give you a peek into each of the creative environments and then walk you through the creation of a *KidPix* slide show.

KidPix Studio Components

KidPix Studio is actually several programs under the one general heading. (You know: The way elementary teachers actually are required to be experts in at least as many areas.) The six mini-programs included on *KidPix Studio* are *KidPix, Moopies, Stampimator, Digital Puppets, Wacky TV,* and *SlideShow.*

My favorite aspect of *KidPix Studio* is the *SlideShow*. Anything you create in each of the other five areas can be incorporated, complete with sound effects and transitions, into a linear slide presentation.

I'm going to give you a quick peek into each of the five artistic components of *KidPix Studio* and then take you, step-by-step, through the creation of a slide show.

KidPix

As I mentioned, *KidPix* is probably the most well-known and highly regarded piece of children's software on the market. One aspect of *KidPix* that I love is that most of the tools used in this program are similar to — if not the same as — the ones artists use when they work with higher-end computer graphics software. If you've never played with *KidPix,* find some time to sit down and experiment with it.

A look at the *KidPix* screen shows you how user-friendly this environment really is: Along the left side of the screen, you see the tools you can use to create your masterpiece. Below the tools, you see a color palette. This color palette has seven sets of coordinated colors — simply click the arrows at the bottom to view a new palette.

Tools

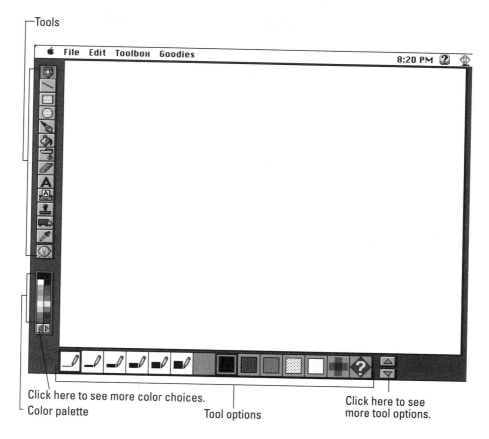

Click here to see more color choices.
Color palette
Tool options
Click here to see more tool options.

Across the bottom of the screen, you see a row of tool options. Not only do you get to choose the type of tool you use and the color you'll be working with, but you also get to choose how you want your tool to work. The options vary from tool to tool. For example, with the paint brush as your tool, you may want the spray paint effect or the effect of dribbled paint lines. The option choices are incredibly wide and varied.

After you have finished your masterpiece, be sure to save by going to the good ol' File menu and choosing Save.

Here are some *KidPix* tips:

✔ While holding down the Shift key, using the line tool produces a straight line or angle; using the rectangle tool produces a perfect square; and using the oval tool produces a perfect circle.

✔ Holding down the Option key while using the oval or rectangle tool will add a thick border to the shape produced. Holding down the ⌘ and Option keys while using the circle or square tool will add an even thicker border to your shape.

✔ Try the Shift, Option, Control, and ⌘ keys for extra effects when using the Wacky Brush or Electric Mixer.

✔ You can resize the stamps you choose by holding down the Shift, Option, and ⌘ keys.

✔ The Eyedropper provides a cool way to figure out what color you used in another part of your picture. Simply click the Eyedropper on the color you want to grab. The color you clicked in the picture will then appear in the current color box at the top of the Paint Palette.

✔ Use the Undo Guy immediately after you make a mistake. He will only undo the last action taken.

Moopies

Moopies are great fun. In the *Moopies* mode, some of the lines you draw will remain as they looked when you created them, although others will begin to jump and wiggle the moment your hand leaves the mouse. The tools are the same as those tools that appear in the regular *KidPix* environment; but in *Moopies,* many of the tools have a life of their own.

There is one added tool in the tool palette — the Dancing Alphabet Text tool. Each of the letters in this alphabet has a special movement or dance. (My students and I used this tool to create the logo for our daily news broadcast.)

Have fun playing in this environment. (My kids love to use the Rain that's part of the Wacky Brush.) When you're ready to stop, it's best to save your work (from the File menu) as a QuickTime movie for use later in a SlideShow.

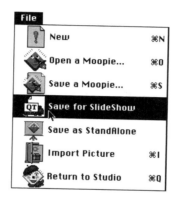

Here are some *Moopies* tips:

> ✔ The Shift, Option, Control, and ⌘ keys will create even crazier effects with the Wacky Brush.

> ✔ It usually works best if you have children draw all their standard straight-line pictures first and then add the "Moopie features" as accents to their masterpieces.

Stampimator

The *Stampimator* workplace looks a little different from the way the *KidPix* and *Moopies* arenas look; the *Stampimator* workplace acts a little differently, too. In the *Stampimator* workplace, the tools down the left and across and the paint palette should look familiar to you. However, as you've probably already noticed, the strip across the bottom already has stamps showing. The icons going down the right side of the screen may seem a little confusing, too! Don't fret; I'll explain them soon. Using *Stampimator* is fun.

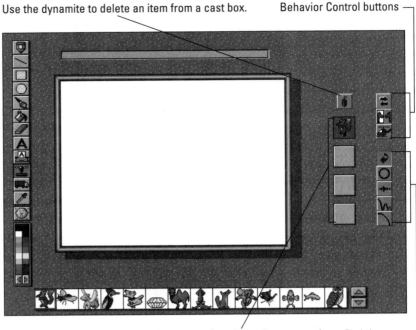

Use the dynamite to delete an item from a cast box.   Behavior Control buttons

Cast boxes (maximum four stamps)   Path buttons

The stamps appear to be the same as those stamps you'll find in *KidPix* or *Moopies*. But guess what? In each of your *Stampimator* pictures, up to four of your chosen stamps can become animated!

My advice, once again, is to have your students create their picture first and then, after studying the elements of the picture, decide where animation might add more interest.

Animating a stamp is simple:

1. If the Stamp Tool isn't already selected, select (click) it.

2. Click inside the first of the four empty boxes on the right side of the screen. These empty boxes are called *cast boxes*.

   Now, click on a Rubber Stamp to select it.

3. Now comes the fun part! While holding down the mouse button, move the stamp wherever you'd like to create the animation you'd like to see on your screen.

   The bar at the top of your picture tells you how much time you've used up. When your time expires, you have reached the end of that stamp's animation path. Let go of the mouse and watch your creation!

Here are some *Stampimator* tips:

✔ To delete a stamp from your picture, click inside the cast box of the stamp you'd like to get rid of and then click the dynamite icon above the row of cast boxes.

✔ Using the Behavior Control buttons allows you to control the motion of your stamps during the Stampimation.

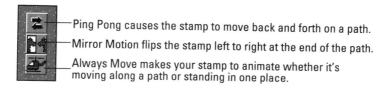

Ping Pong causes the stamp to move back and forth on a path.

Mirror Motion flips the stamp left to right at the end of the path.

Always Move makes your stamp to animate whether it's moving along a path or standing in one place.

✔ The Path buttons also allow you to assert a little control over the picture. The default setting for these buttons is always Original path (the path you created when you moved the stamp). The other settings create the following movements:

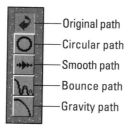

Original path

Circular path

Smooth path

Bounce path

Gravity path

✔ If you plan to use this creation in the *SlideShow* that I'll show you how to create later in this chapter, be sure to save it as a QuickTime movie.

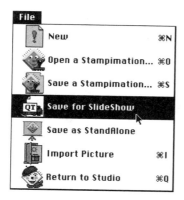

Digital Puppets

I see the *Digital Puppets* as more of a fun diversion than as an educational enhancement. However, I guess kids could create digital puppets and have them introduce a presentation or project. Try the puppets out and see what you think.

Record your puppet's movements.

Stop

Pause

Playback

This area of *KidPix Studio* is straightforward:

1. You choose your puppet by going to the Goodies menu. (You can choose from ten different puppets.)

2. To move the puppets, you simply type on the keyboard. Every puppet is programmed with a limited set of movements, so experiment and see what movements you come up with.

3. When you like the combination of movements you've put together, press the red button at the bottom of your screen to record your puppet show.

Here are some *Digital Puppets* tips to try from the Goodies menu:

✔ Adding a sound to the background can make your show lots of fun to create and watch. Why not choose a nice tango and have Peteroo the Kangaroo move in time to the music?

✔ You'll find that most of the puppets have keys that correspond to mouth movements. I like to record an introductory message and then try to make the puppet's mouth move to correspond with my recorded message.

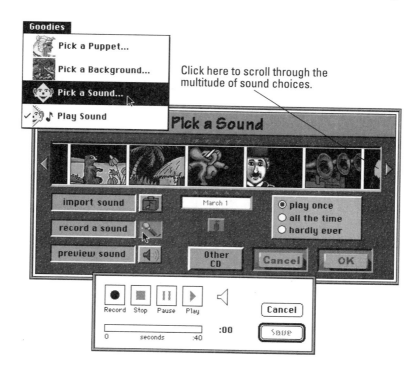

Click here to scroll through the multitude of sound choices.

Wacky TV

Wacky TV is nothing more than a silly screen on which you can play any of the QuickTime movies that you've created in the other areas of *KidPix Studio*, movies that come with *KidPix Studio*, or any commercially produced movies you've purchased.

Play   Quit   Step by step   Electric
    Stop   Channel changer   Rewind   Mixer

1. You can get some funky effects added to your movie by clicking the Electric Mixer icon at the bottom of the TV screen. After clicking the mixer, you'll see eight new icons appear at the bottom of the screen along with the Undo Guy.

2. Play around with the special effects that occur when you select each of these new icons.

3. Okay, before you turn into a real couch potato (or should I say computer potato?), click the Hand icon and return to the main menu.

A Word about Backgrounds

The number of backgrounds available within *KidPix Studio* is amazing. You can add backgrounds while you're working with *Moopies, Stampimator,* or *Digital Puppets.* Simply go to the Goodies menu and choose Pick a Background.

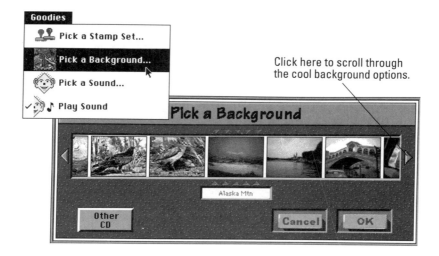

Click here to scroll through the cool background options.

Scroll through the backgrounds until you see the one you like, or click Other CD to import purchased background artwork from another CD, and then click OK.

Check out Appendix B for easy-to-access visual guides to all the backgrounds available in *KidPix Studio.*

Sounds Abound

Importing sounds is a great way to make use of the multimedia capabilities of this program. This option is only available while working with *Moopies, Stampimator,* or *Digital Puppets.*

To add a sound, choose Pick a Sound from the Goodies menu.

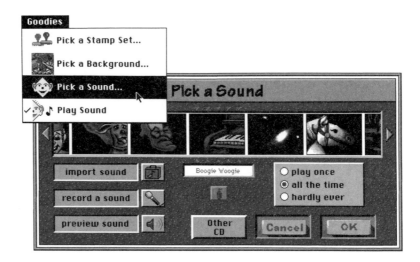

This dialog box gives you an amazing amount of freedom. You can choose from the batch of sounds that *KidPix Studio* has graciously provided for you (my personal favorite is Boogie Woogie), record your own sound (it's as simple as operating a classroom tape recorder), or even import a sound from another CD (remember the copyright laws). You also have the choice of how often you want the sound to play — once, all the time, or hardly ever.

Check out Appendix B for a list of all the sounds available within *KidPix Studio.*

Photo-CD Capabilities

The programmers at Brøderbund don't miss a beat. In addition to all the stuff you've just read about, *KidPix Studio* is also Kodak-Photo-CD compatible. This quite simply means that any images that you have stored on a Kodak Photo CD can be pulled into a *KidPix* picture or opened as backgrounds in any of your *Moopies, Stampimator,* or *Digital Puppets* creations.

Creating an Award-Winning SlideShow

If you haven't created and saved (be sure to use the Save for SlideShow option) a couple of masterpieces, go ahead, have some fun, and come back to this section later.

1. Click the *SlideShow* icon on the main menu.

   You should now see a confusing bunch of moving vans. Your mission, should you choose to accept it, is to fill two of these vans with pictures you've created.

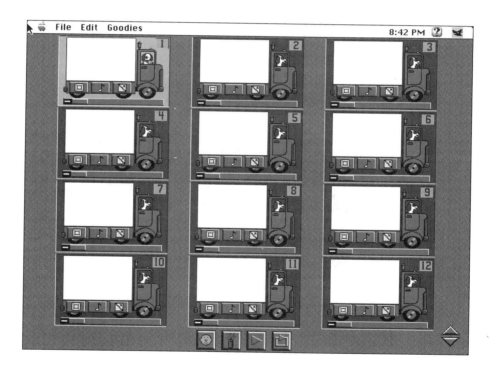

2. Click the picture frame at the base of the first truck.

   A screen pops up and tells you to Pick a Picture. You should see a list of all your beautiful creations.

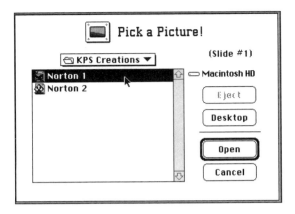

3. Choose a picture and click Open.

   Your picture should now be loaded in the first truck. Go ahead and load your other picture(s) into the other trucks.

4. Now we get to add some sound! See the musical note at the base of the trucks? Click the note on the first truck. Another dialog box should pop into view requesting that you Pick a Sound.

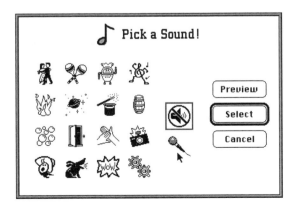

Play around with the different sound choices or record your own sound effects. When you've got the sound you want, click Select. (If you loaded a picture that already had sound attached, the musical note will be shaded, and you won't be given the choice of adding a sound.) Add sounds to each of the trucks.

The last square at the base of each truck is for your transition choice. The *transition* takes you from one slide or picture to another.

5. If you choose the scissors icon in the Pick a Transition dialog box, the transition will be quick. Choose any of the others to get some really neat special effects. Pick a transition for each truck.

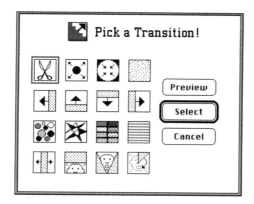

You've done it! You're show is complete. You'll know whether you made all the necessary choices if each icon/picture, sound, and transition square becomes filled with color. To view the *SlideShow*, press the arrow at the bottom of the screen.

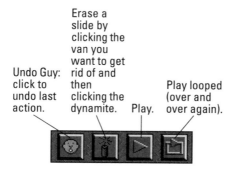

6. You can save your show or simply choose Quit from the File menu.

Take a look at Chapter 12 for some great ideas for incorporating *KidPix Studio* into your everyday curriculum.

KidPix Studio Saving Solutions

Here's a quick-and-dirty rundown of what each of the confusing Save options means:

Save: Using this option allows you to reopen the file in the environment in which it was originally created. If you use this option, you'll have to have *KidPix Studio* on the view the computer will be using.

Save for SlideShow: Using this option saves your file as a QuickTime movie, which makes it easy to import the file into a slide show with all of its elements (sound, movement, and graphics) intact.

Save as StandAlone: Using this option saves your file with all the information needed to run it without having *KidPix Studio* installed on the computer on which it will be viewed. If your creations are small enough, you can then save them to a floppy disk and send the disk to friends, family, or other schools.

Well, that's an overview of *KidPix Studio.* I think that you'll find plenty within this program to keep younger students busy and creative throughout the school year. In the following chapter, I'll take you through the steps involved in creating a presentation using *HyperStudio* — the gem of multimedia presentation programs.

Chapter 10
Faking It Through *HyperStudio*

In This Chapter
▶ The lowdown on *HyperStudio*
▶ How to make a *HyperStudio* stack
▶ How to add buttons and sound to your *HyperStudio* stuff
▶ Even more ideas on using *HyperStudio*

*T*here is no possible way to expose all the many facets of *HyperStudio* within this one small chapter. Whole books have been devoted to the subject!

As I've mentioned before, the neat thing about writing for educators is that I already know how intelligent and innovative you are. Teachers can take a small morsel of information and turn it into a huge meal.

So let's get cooking!

The Big Picture

Before we even get into the program, I want to try and explain the overall scheme. I must admit that the name of this program is a little overwhelming to the novice Mac user. So let's first get a mental image of what it is that you are about to create.

Electronic index cards

HyperStudio is all about "stacks" of cards. Imagine those trusty little 3 × 5-inch index cards. (I sometimes use these same cards to help students visualize the process of creating a *HyperStudio* presentation.)

With *HyperStudio,* you create stacks of cards that can be linked together to create an *interactive presentation.* This all sounds very highbrow, but in reality creating stacks is as simple as building those story webs you've all created to show the relationships between different aspects of a story.

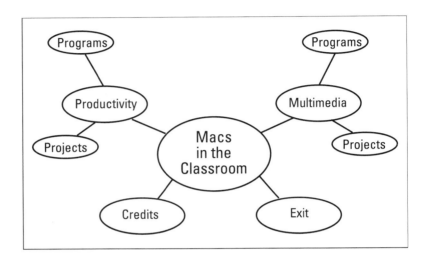

Webs become cards

Each part of the web, including the title, would be a card in *HyperStudio.* By adding buttons to each card, you can let the viewer choose a path through the presentation.

For example, the title card *Macs in the Classroom* might have four buttons: one for Productivity, one for Multimedia, one for Credits, and one to Exit the program. After clicking the Multimedia button, you'd see a screen with some information and two more buttons: Programs and Projects. While viewing the stack, there would also be buttons letting you go back to the main menu and access other areas of the stack. Get the picture? Using *HyperStudio* is a way of creating a personalized, interactive learning tool. If you think about it, using one of these interactive learning tools is very much like using an automatic teller at a bank — you push buttons to decide what action you want to take place.

I know that *HyperStudio* sounds complex, but once you get involved, using *HyperStudio* is addictive. The fun part is creating interesting and informative cards, deciding on transitions between the cards, and adding buttons to link the cards.

Here We Go

I'm now going to take you, step by step, through the creation of a three-card stack on *Macs in the Classroom.*

Card 1

1. Open the *HyperStudio* folder on your Hard Drive. You'll be presented with a window that looks like this:

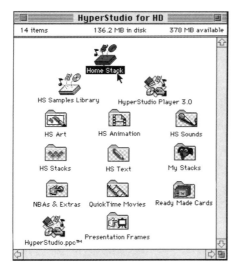

2. Double-click the Home Stack icon. The Home Stack welcome screen comes up. Click the New Stack icon. You'll be asked whether you're sure that you want to leave the Home Stack. Click the Yes button.

As in *KidPix,* you are presented with a blank palette just waiting for your creative additions. Now you are going to create a more user friendly environment.

3. Go to the Tools menu. (The Tools menu is "draggable." As the name implies, you can drag this menu off the menu bar for easy access while you work.)

    Click on the menu and — before letting go — drag the menu to one side of your blank card.

    Now you are ready to get creative! You should recognize many of the tools already — many of them are the same as those tools you just used in *KidPix Studio.* The first card you will make will be the title card or menu card for the stack.

4. From the Edit menu, choose Erase Background.

    A dialog box appears with a strip of beautiful colors. Select a shade of gray and click OK. Did your card turn gray? Gray will continue to be your background color throughout the entire stack unless you change it.

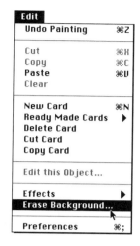

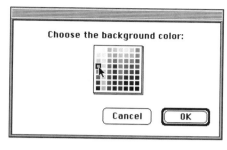

Keeping a consistent background color adds continuity to a stack and gives your stack a more professional look. However, consistent background color is by no means a requirement — let the kids be as creative as they want.

5. Now choose the Rounded Rectangle from the Tools menu.

   Go to the Options menu and choose Line Size. After the dialog box appears, choose the thickest line and click OK.

   Finally, from the Colors menu, choose the brick texture.

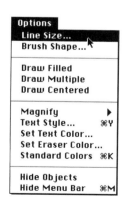

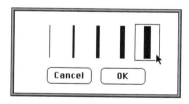

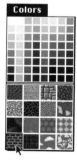

6. Take the crosshairs to the upper-left corner of the card and pull to the lower-right corner of the card. Let go when you think that it looks proportional.

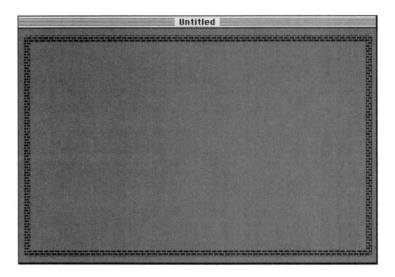

7. Now let's add a picture. From the File menu, choose Add Clip Art. Then select Disk file.

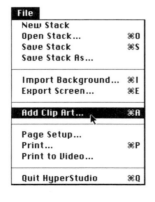

After the following dialog boxes appears, choose Computer 2:

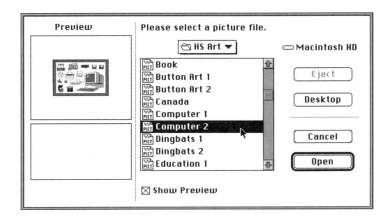

8. After the image appears, click the Lasso tool. Encircle the large computer image while pressing the mouse button.

   After you release the mouse button, the image of the computer will shimmer. (When a graphic is highlighted, it appears this way.) Click OK.

Shimmering after being encircled with the lasso.

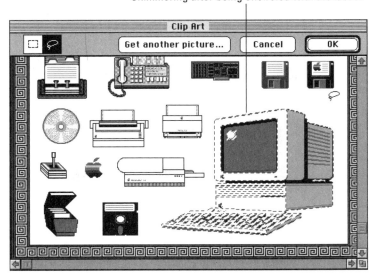

The image of the computer should appear on your card. A strange icon, looking something like a compass rose, appears where the lasso used to be. This icon means you are free to move the image anywhere on the screen. Move the image to the right-center side of your card by dragging it; then click outside your image. You've now placed your first piece of clip art!

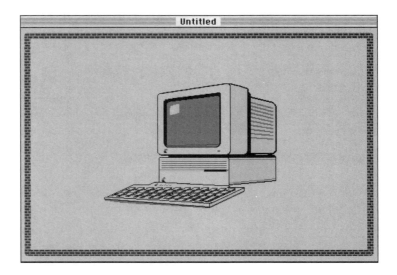

9. Now let's add the title of your stack to this first card. Choose Text Style from the Options menu.

   After the dialog box appears, choose the font, style, size, and color of your choice and click OK.

   (I chose Helvetica, Bold, 48pt., and black.)

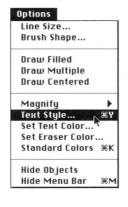
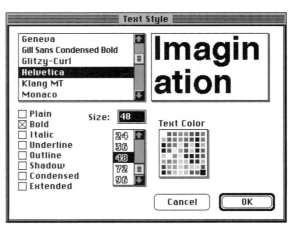

10. From the Tools menu, choose the T. Your pointer changes to an I-beam cursor.

Put the I-beam in the upper-left corner of your screen and click. Type **Macs** and press Return. Type **in the** and press Return. Finally, type **Classroom**. (I also added a byline in another font.)

Congratulations! You've created your first card!

Card 2

1. Go to the Edit menu and choose New Card.

   Another blank card should appear with a gray background. This card is going to give the viewer (the person who will ultimately use your creation) some information on multimedia computing.

   Go to the File menu and choose Add Clip Art. Then select Disk file.

2. After the dialog box appears, choose Computer 1.

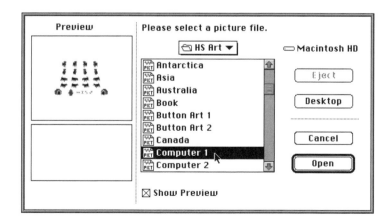

This time, use the Rectangle tool (which gives you crosshairs for selection) and choose the image of the man at the computer. Click OK when you are finished. Position the image in the upper-left corner of your card. Before you click off the image to place it, try dragging the edges to enlarge it either horizontally or vertically — you'll know that it's okay to enlarge after the double-headed arrow appears. Click off the image after the image is the size you want and in the position you want it to be.

"Marching ants" show you
what area has been chosen.

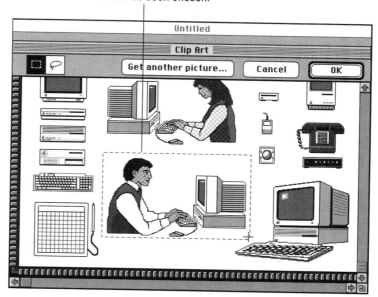

Pull here to enlarge or reduce.

3. You're going to add some information about multimedia computing to the right side of the screen.

From the Objects menu, select Add a Text Object. You'll see a confusing instruction screen, but just click OK — I'm giving the instructions here!

The text block (where you're eventually going to see text) appears on the screen. You can move the text block by pressing down on the mouse button and dragging to the right side of the screen. You can change the size of the text block by dragging at its corners, its top, or its bottom. Click outside the box to place it.

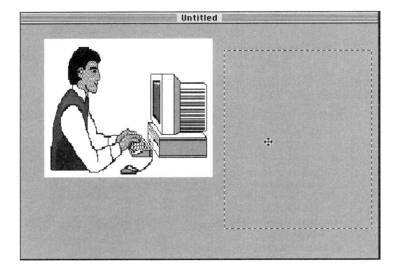

4. Yet another dialog box appears! Click the Style button. Choose Helvetica, Bold, 24pt.

You can also make these choices: Align (left), Text Color (yellow), and Background (black). Click OK.

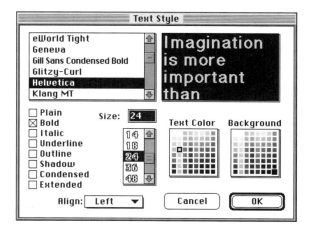

5. Back to that first dialog box! In the name box, type **Multimedia**.

Now let's decide which boxes you need to "x" at the bottom of this box. Choose these options: Draw scroll bar and Scrollable. Click OK.

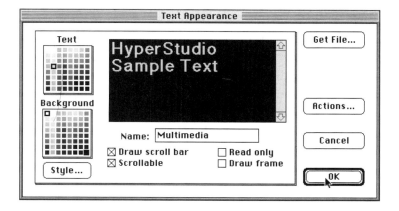

6. Now type your information in the box. Don't worry if you run out of room; the box will scroll for you to continue typing. Type four sentences about multimedia computing.

Great! Just one more card to go!

Card 3

1. Go to the Edit menu and choose New Card. Once again you are given a blank card with a gray background.

   I'm tired of gray. How about you? Go to the Edit menu and choose Erase Background. Go wild — choose any color you'd like.

2. Go to the File menu again and choose Add Clip Art. After your choices appear, choose Computer 1 again. This time, however, use the Lasso tool and encircle the woman at the computer.

   Click OK. The image should appear on your card.

   Now it's time to learn a new skill, boys and girls. I want this image to be huge! No, you can't feed her chocolate cake and bonbons, but you can use a nifty trick called *scaling.* Your image of the computing woman should still be shimmering, because you haven't yet placed her on the card.

3. Move the lasso onto the image. It turns into that compass-rose thing. Now go to the Edit menu and choose Effects. When you slide to the right of the word *Effects,* you'll see Scale as one of your choices. Choose it.

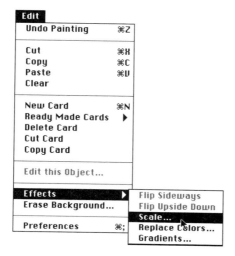

4. Of course, you see a new dialog box. (I think that these things reproduce within the Mac!) This dialog box tells you that your friend is currently appearing at 100%. But you want more! Change that percentage to 160%.

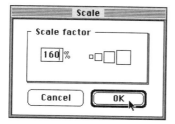

Click OK and watch your friend grow! Now, before you click outside of the image (and stop the shimmering), move her to the right side of your card. Click outside of the image. She is now in place.

5. Now you need to add some text. From the Objects menu, choose Add Text Object.

You remember how to add text, right? Position your text block in the upper-left corner of the card. Don't make this text block too large.

Click off the text block. Your Text Appearance dialog box appears. Click the style button and choose Helvetica, Bold, 18pt., Text Color (black), and the Background color of your choice. (Let's not clash with our card background, though!)

Finally choose Center alignment. Click OK.

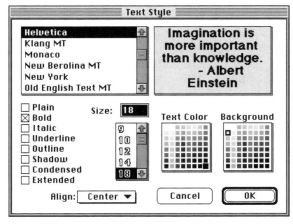

8. Name this text **Productivity** and click the Draw frame box. (Make sure that all of the others are blank.) Click OK and type your info in the box.

And, my friends, you are finished creating your cards. Now comes the exciting part — adding buttons!

Button Your Cards!

HyperStudio gives you the power of interactive buttons. *Buttons* are specially-formatted areas of the screen that, when clicked, perform programmed actions (go to another card, play a movie, play a sound, perform animation) or a combination of any of these actions. This capability is what makes *HyperStudio* an incredible program. This capability is also why your friend, the business person, is using this program (and others like it that cost a great deal more) to create presentations for use in the "real world."

1. Go to the Move menu and choose First Card.

   Now go to the Objects menu and choose Add a Button. Guess what? You'll see a dialog box!

Move

Back	⌘~
Home	⌘H
First Card	⌘1
Previous Card	⌘<
Next Card	⌘>
Last Card	⌘9
Jump To Card...	⌘J
Find Text...	⌘F

Objects

Add a Button...	⌘B
Add a Graphic Object...	⌘G
Add a Text Object...	⌘T
Hypertext Links...	⌘L
Bring Closer	⌘+
Send Farther	⌘-
About this Card...	
About this Stack...	

2. You want your first button to take you to the Multimedia card. So type **Multimedia** in the Name area (it should be highlighted, so just start typing).

To the left of this dialog box, you should see a variety of shapes. Choose the one at the top right. On the right side of the box, you see a beautiful array of colors. The top choices are for text color on the button. Let's just leave it black. The bottom choices are for background color on the button. Choose white. Your final choices appear in the bottom-left corner of the box.

Trust me. Choose Show Name and Highlight. Click OK.

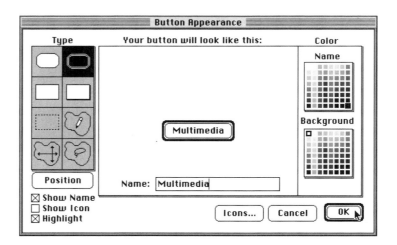

3. A very informative screen (with too much text) appears telling you to select where you want to place your button. Click OK and then put your cursor on top of the button (the edges should be shimmering). Once again, you get that little strange-looking thing.

Move the button to position just under the title; then click off the button.

4. Oh, my gosh! Another dialog box! This dialog box (and a couple more that follow) are really loads of fun. They allow you to control what happens when this new button is pressed.

   On the left side of the screen, choose Next Card.

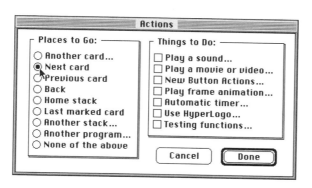

5. You now have to decide the type of transition (With cross-fade, Dissolve, and so on) that you want to see when this card switches to the next one. Yes, there is a Try it button. So go crazy. Try them all.

   After you've found that perfect transition (my favorite is Dissolve), highlight it and choose the Speed. Then click OK.

   Wasn't that fun?

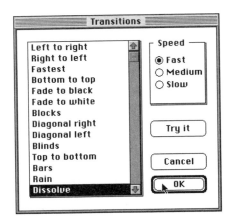

6. On the right side of the screen, choose Play a Sound.

   The dialog box in front of you now is the last one you must suffer through in order to create this button. This is a pretty cool-looking dialog box now, isn't it? What you decide here is the sound that will be made when your button is clicked.

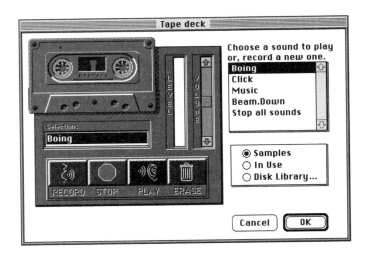

7. You could be very average and highlight Click and be done with it. But not you; you're a computing fool . . . you want more! Choose Disk Library in the lower box.

8. You now have an incredible selection of sounds to choose from. And guess what? Korg has a very funky New Age computer sound. Choose it and click Open.

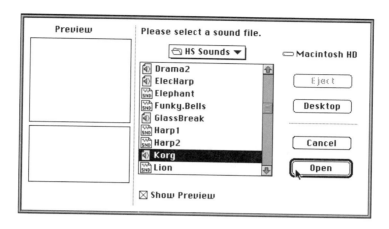

The Korg sound is now loaded in the tape recorder. Click Play to hear this New Age funk; then click OK if the sound meets with your approval. It's silly of me to ask you to choose it now because I know that you are going to spend the next ten minutes going through all of the sounds and listening to them. (You can even buy additional sounds!) Yes, we can also act like kids if we want to. (Go ahead; I won't tell anyone.)

9. Before *HyperStudio* will place your button, it will ask you to name your stack. Call it **Classroom Computers**.

10. You've made your first button. Now make another one by following these same steps with the following exceptions: Place it below the Multimedia button and name this new button **Productivity**.

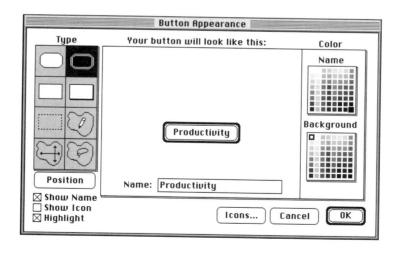

11. After the Button Actions screen appears, choose Another card from the Places to Go section.

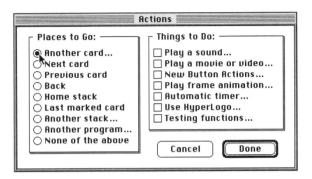

The next screen tells you to use the arrows to find the card that you want to connect with. Click the right arrow until you come to the Productivity card; then click OK.

12. Next you'll be asked to choose your transition — just like before. Choose the Korg sound from the disk library. Click OK.

Click Done on the next screen that you see.

13. In order to test your buttons, you'll have to choose the Browse tool, which looks like a hand. You'll find it in the Tools menu.

Go ahead, click the Multimedia button. Did you move to the next card?

Even teachers make mistakes

I guess this is as good a time as any to tell you how to make a correction to a button or simply how to delete the little rascal and start all over. Correcting and deleting buttons are actually very easy tasks. Go to the Tools menu. Do you see the little button in the center of the top row? Choose it. Now drag your cursor on top of your button.

It should begin to shimmer — that means the button is selected. If you want to get rid of this button, press the Delete key now. If you simply want to alter its appearance or change its actions, double-click. You'll be given all the original button options. *Très facile?*

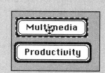

Make Your Button Talk!

You're probably tired of buttons. Trod on a little farther — you'll be glad you did.

1. I hope that you are now on the Multimedia card. If not, go to the Move menu and choose First Card. From there, use your great little button.

2. We need to create two buttons on this card: one to take you back to the title card and one to read the text out loud.

   The first one is easy. Go to the Objects menu. Choose Add a Button. This time, rather than choosing Show Name and Highlight, choose Show Icon. You will then be shown a selection of icons.

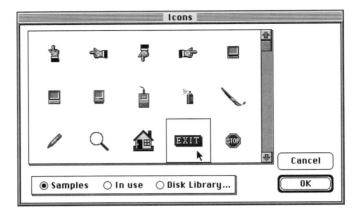

Choose the Exit sign. Click OK.

3. Now choose the box with the dotted outline in the Type menu. Click OK; place the button in the lower-left corner of your card.

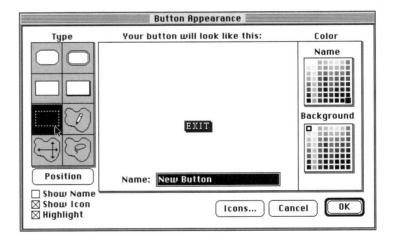

4. Click outside the card. The Button Actions box appears.

   Choose Another Card and use the left arrow to go back to the first card.

   Then pick a transition and click OK.

   Finally, choose Play a Sound and pick your sound. Click OK. This button is complete.

5. If your Mac has a microphone, the next button you make will be a talkie. That's right! Choose Add a Button from the Objects menu. (And they said that rote memorization was a thing of the past; it's working for you.) If you don't have a microphone, see the "Where's the microphone?" sidebar in this chapter.

This time, choose the button shape in the bottom-left corner as your Type and then click OK. You are actually creating an invisible button. Addy (the dog) comes on, telling you to create a shape for your button. Click OK and then click inside the text block.

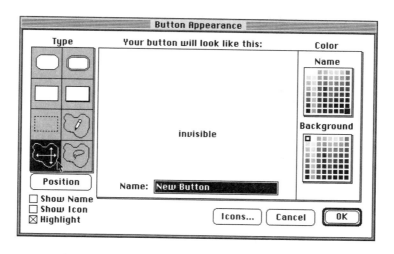

After Addy comes back — telling you that your button's shape has been defined — click OK.

6. This button is going to trigger a recording of your voice reading the text, so choose None of the above in the Places to Go box.

In the Things to Do box, choose Play a sound.

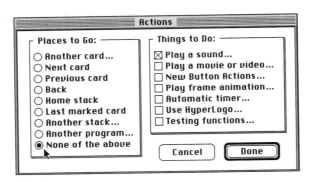

The tape recorder pops up ready for you to use. Push Record and read the text. Push Stop when you've finished.

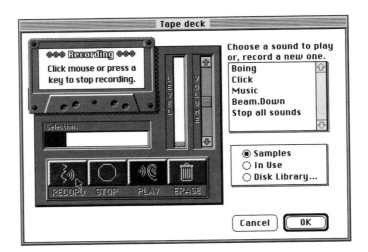

Use the play button to see whether you like your reading; then click OK. Click Done on the next screen — and try out that button. Remember, the button is invisible, so just click anywhere on your text block. You should hear yourself reading!

Where's the microphone?

A Macintosh microphone has a microphone icon on the end of its cord that plugs into the microphone jack on the back of the computer (although some Macs do have built-in microphones). Apple makes two types of microphones.

If a microphone isn't attached to your computer, ask whether someone in your school has the microphones stored somewhere. (We don't leave microphones on the computers in our lab—when we do, the microphones tend to disappear.)

You're on Your Own

I'm going to let you use your creative talents to create the button(s) for the last card. You'll need at least one to take you back to the title card. Have faith . . . you can do this. Look back at the previous directions if you need some reminders.

Quitting

I'm sure that you're already thinking of all the stacks you or your class could make. But there comes a time (usually around 4:00 every afternoon) when we all must quit for the day. This program is just like any other program. Go to File and choose Save Stack. If you are saving this stack on your hard drive, just type in a name for your stack and click Save. Your stack will be nestled comfortably in the *HyperStudio* folder until you return.

If you want to save this stack to a disk, choose Save from the File menu. After the dialog box appears, insert your disk in the drive and name your stack. Click the Save button.

Note: Some of the features in *HyperStudio* take up a great deal of space on a disk. Making a few small stacks and linking them together with buttons is better than making one huge stack.

Ideas That Work Great for HyperStudio Stacks

I'm sure you'll find tons of ways to use *HyperStudio* across the curriculum. Here are a few of my favorites:

- ✔ stacks of math problems with buttons connecting to answer cards
- ✔ meet our school faculty — a card with audio about each VIP in your school
- ✔ vacation guide — something in which to import photos, maps, and movies
- ✔ endangered species — a stack for each species with branching cards telling vital information
- ✔ state or country report — a commercial for your state with each card highlighting different aspects
- ✔ classroom scrapbook — an ongoing project as the school year progresses
- ✔ family history — scanned photos from home with actual recorded voices of family members
- ✔ your own *e-books* (electronic books) — invisible buttons could control characters' voices

See Chapter 12 for more great ideas. And take a look at the sample projects *HyperStudio* included on the *Mac Multimedia For Teachers CD*.

Top Ten HyperStudio Tips

As I mentioned before, whole books have been written on *HyperStudio,* but here are a few of my favorite pointers:

1. **Keep your buttons consistent.**

   In other words, if you have a card on each button that takes the user back to the menu card, make sure that you use the exact same button each time. This arrangement makes it less confusing for the person viewing your stack.

2. **Make all changes to text entered on your background (not the text blocks) before you click away from the area.**

   Even though what you've typed appears as text, what you've typed is actually working as a graphic item when it's not in the text block. Therefore, making corrections is almost impossible without actually erasing it first and retyping.

3. Share your stacks with others.

If you're creative, you owe it to the rest of us. If you're not so creative (like me), act like a sponge and soak up all the good ideas you see!

4. Plan ahead.

This tip makes all the difference in the world. One side of the Cheat Sheet found in the front of this book has a copy of the planning sheet I use when creating *HyperStudio* stacks and *KidPix Studio* slide shows.

5. Use invisible (non-text) buttons when creating stacks for younger children who may be non-readers.

That way, just about anywhere they click, something will happen.

6. Try some of the Ready Made Cards found in the Edit menu.

My favorite is the Storybook Page.

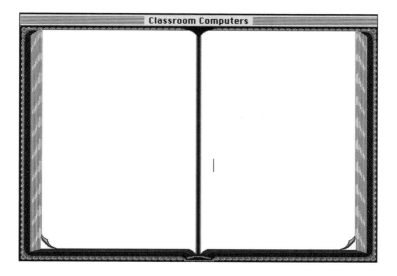

7. Use the StoryBoard feature found in the Extra menu to preview all the cards you've created.

Within the storyboard, you can rearrange the order of your cards or delete unwanted cards.

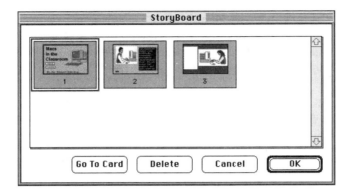

8. Use the Preferences option found in the Edit menu to make your stack look more professional.

Make sure that the Show Card Number with Stack Name is unchecked and make sure that the Presentation Mode box is checked. When you check the Presentation mode box, yet another dialog box will appear. This time you'll want to choose a color for the desktop while your presentation is playing and make sure that the Show the title bar box is unchecked. Then click OK.

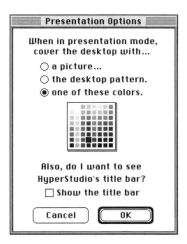

9. **Print your cards on paper.**

Doing so helps younger students visualize the stack and organize their
button functions. Choose Print under the File menus. You'll be given the
option of printing one, two, or four cards per page.

10. **Think before choosing your artwork.**

Clip art and graphic items may appear to be the same thing. However, clip
art becomes a part of your background, and graphic items float above the
background. "So what?" you ask. Well, if you try to erase or move a piece
of clip art, you'll lose part of your background. You will have to go back
and refill that area. A graphic item simply floats over the background and
can be moved without disturbing what's underneath.

Other Cool Stuff You Can Do with HyperStudio

I've only scratched the surface when it comes to the cool stuff you can do with *HyperStudio*. Take a look at the sample stacks provided with the *HyperStudio* demo on the *Mac Multimedia For Teachers CD*. The following list contains a few of the other *HyperStudio* capabilities that you'll probably want to learn about:

- ✔ insert movies
- ✔ insert photo CD pictures
- ✔ import scanned images
- ✔ create animation
- ✔ roll credits on a final card (just like the movies)
- ✔ import clip art from other sources (you can buy CDs full of clip art and background designs)

Your *HyperStudio* manual has all the information you need to complete these tasks — and much more; what I've given you here barely scratches the surface. Learn and become comfortable with the basics. Then branch out on your own, you multimedia marvel!

HyperStudio Resources

I hit a gold mine when I pulled up *HyperStudio* on America Online. *HyperStudio's* keyword is **StudioWare**.

After you get to the *HyperStudio* forum, you can wander around the bulletin board to see answers to commonly asked questions. You can also get some really neat stacks (stacks that others, such as you, decided to share with the rest of the online world).

I also discovered some very informative *HyperStudio* newsletters that are available on a quarterly basis (on disks); they contain hints, ideas, clip art, sounds, button artwork, and much more. I learned quite a bit from the samples I downloaded.

Here's the critical info for the newsletters I viewed:

- ✔ ***HyperStudio Network:*** For $29 a year, you get a quarterly newsletter (*HyperStudio Forum*), a *Best of HyperStudio* disk, and discounts on products, studioware, and other hypermedia materials. (See the insert that comes with your *HyperStudio* software.)

- ✔ ***HyperStudio Journal:*** For $45 a year ($10 each for back issues), you get a bimonthly publication from Simtech Publications, 134 East Street, Litchfield, CT 06759. A sample issue of *HyperStudio Journal* can be found on the *Mac Multimedia For Teachers CD*.

The 5th Wave — By Rich Tennant

"The system came bundled with a CD-ROM drive, a sound card, and the developer's out of work nephew."

Chapter 11
Making the Curriculum Connection

In This Chapter

▶ Planning ideas for multimedia presentations

▶ Know what you can do

▶ Lay it out

*H*ealth has always been one of those subjects that I've slighted when time was tight and something had to be cut. Go ahead and admit it: You've done it, too. There's just not enough time in the day to cover all subjects the way you'd like or the way your students deserve. I once taught in a school that had the foresight to hire a health teacher. This person saw my class once a week and was able to cover all the required health objectives and do a really good job — not to mention that this plan freed up more time for me to spend covering other subjects. (It also relieved a great deal of the guilt I felt each time that I just *had* to let a lesson slide.)

Teachers tend to view technology as another lesson, similar to health or social studies, that they just don't have time to fit in. However, through the use of multimedia projects, a little planning, and some great software, they can make better use of their classroom time than they'd ever imagined.

What's the Plan?

Plans are important. We've all (or the majority of us) become painfully aware of this fact at least once in our illustrious teaching careers. You know what I'm talking about: The one morning that your child decides to vomit as you're walking out the door just happens to be the morning that your plans are in your school bag (at home) and not on your desk!

Planning for multimedia activities is just as important as planning for regular classroom lessons — and just as easy.

Before you begin, however, I think that this would be a great time for you to take a look at some of the sample presentations provided by *Hyperstudio* on the *Mac Multimedia For Teachers CD*. Seeing these examples will help you better visualize the planning involved and the activities mentioned later in the chapter.

Know Your Limitations

Before embarking on your great multimedia journey, take inventory of your stock. Find out what you've got to work with and how much time you have; and don't forget to take into account both your capabilities and your students' capabilities.

Computers, peripherals, and software

Before you get started, be sure to do the following:

- ✔ Make lists of all equipment you have access to, including computers, scanners, digital cameras, video equipment, CD-ROMs, laser discs, input devices, and the like.
- ✔ Take note of memory requirements.
- ✔ Make sure that the software you plan to use is compatible with your computer setup.

Keep all of this information in mind as you decide on the direction you plan to take with your first multimedia project. Make good use of what you have on hand and don't make plans that you won't be able to finish because you don't have the necessary equipment.

Time, time, time

There's never enough time in a day or, for that matter, in the school year. Don't make the mistake of going headfirst into a multimedia project before making sure that you can devote the time needed to finish the project.

- ✔ Decide what curriculum area you are ready to focus on and devote that classroom time to working on the multimedia project. Remember, technology should compliment the curriculum, not be a separate curriculum itself.
- ✔ Set aside time for research and planning. Sign up with your media specialist if necessary.

✔ Sign up for lab time or arrange for access to computers in your classroom.

✔ Check your calendar. You know how busy certain months can become. December and May are quickly filled with holiday and end-of-the-year activities. Don't begin a multimedia project that you may not be able to finish in a reasonable amount of time.

Be honest with yourself

All this means is don't bite off more than you can chew. Start small on your first project and do a good job. Become comfortable with all the equipment you have and use it all. Then the next time around, you'll be ready to attempt bigger and better projects.

You also need to be sure that your students are trained on the equipment you'll be using. Otherwise, valuable project time will be spent teaching equipment use, and you'll soon find yourself behind schedule.

Laying It All Out

Well, now that you're painfully aware of your limitations, you still want to go for it. You've decided what curriculum area to focus on, and you've set aside research and computer time. Now let's map out your route.

Clearly state your expectations

After you've decided on a unit or subject area, make a plan of action that is very specific. List your goals and desired outcome and, above all, map out a criteria for grading the project. I'll leave these decisions up to you. All teachers have their own beliefs about the grading system, and you probably have local school requirements that you must follow as well.

Honor that style!

Don't forget about individual learning styles. Encourage students to pursue areas of multimedia research and development that enable them to share their knowledge in a way that best suits them. I'm sure those nonartistic types (like me) would welcome the assistance of a spatial learner. After all, we are all seeking to give students the best possible education available. In some respects, learning styles allow us to do just that.

Work with small groups of students

One great aspect of my new job is being able to work with small groups of students. So much can be accomplished when a few individuals are focused on one common goal. The smaller you can make your groups, the better the final product will be. It also helps to have small groups if you are sending them to other areas of the school to work on research or to use computers. Three well-behaved individuals are usually welcomed with open arms. A band of 10 to 12 students, even if they're well-behaved students, rarely receives the same greeting from a lab assistant or media clerk.

A few design options

I like to use index cards and string to show students exactly how all the cards in a presentation will relate to one another. Even though programs such as *KidPix Studio* and *Multimedia Workshop* are linear and don't require connections, I think that younger students need to see the order of their cards in the presentation.

Other teachers prefer to use storyboards or a combination of storyboards and cards when mapping out their plans. Following are diagrams of some of the more common layout designs for multimedia projects:

Straight Line (right side of the hall, single file)

This plan is the most often used one. You start out with a title page and go through in one direction. When you get to the end, you can start over again.

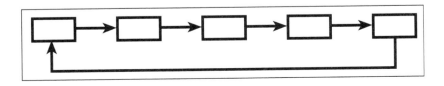

Two-Way Linear (one class is going outside while the other comes inside)

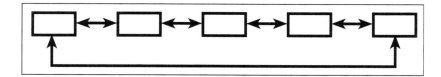

This plan works just like the straight line, except the viewer has the freedom to wander backward through the cards as well as forward.

Indexed Straight Line (the principal calls children into his office according to the severity of their actions)

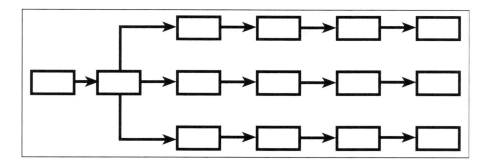

This plan is the first to incorporate the use of a table of contents that usually appears after the title card. From the table of contents, users decide which line of knowledge they will travel.

Treetop (where kids shouldn't be on the playground)

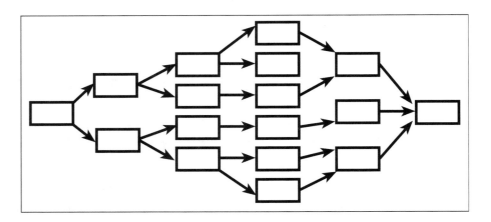

Oh, my goodness. Here we go! At this point, things can start getting tricky, and the string that you've been using on the floor with your index-card example can begin to tangle. The cards or screens in these stacks may have one or more buttons that enable the user to make decisions. Thus, one card can lead in two totally different directions.

Spoke (don't be the cog in the wheel)

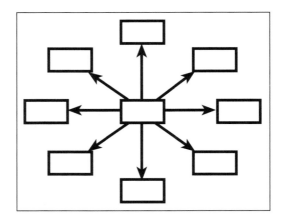

This plan is great for the younger set. It would also be the plan used for a class photo album or class magazine (see Chapter 14). The center card serves as the table of contents or title page. This card contains a button for each of the branches coming off it. In the case of the class magazine, each story would have a button, and the title card would be the table of contents for the magazine.

Grid (please navigate in an orderly fashion)

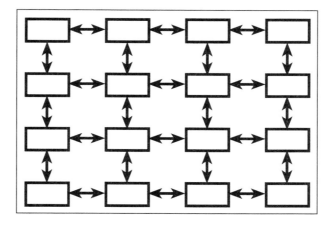

Using a stack of cards in a grid layout is somewhat like navigating a map. The Welcome Wagon project in the next chapter would probably be set up in this manner.

Keep your eye on the prize

Getting carried away with the technology behind a multimedia project is easy. I've often seen students get all caught up in how many ways they can use video or how cool their voices sound when recorded.

There will often be times when you need to re-group and refocus on the goal. Do this regrouping on a regular basis, and you'll achieve the desired results.

Controlled Chaos (my classroom on most days)

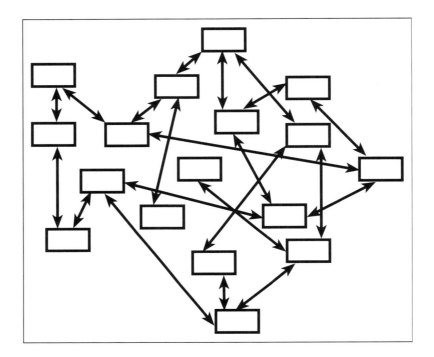

This layout design truly does resemble my classroom on a good day. A lot is going on, and it looks a bit confusing, but all the discussion is *good stuff*. There's real learning going on here. All the cards exist by themselves, yet they are also interrelated in some areas. Encyclopedia CDs use this same setup.

On the Cheat Sheet, you'll find a planning sheet that might also prove helpful when planning your multimedia adventures.

So go ahead and read on. Pick an activity from the next chapter and make all the required plans. Then all that's left to do is go for it!

Chapter 12

Lights, Camera, Action!

· ·

In This Chapter

▶ Lavish language arts presentations

▶ A multitude of math ideas

▶ Sensational social studies stacks

▶ Super science shows

▶ Health happenings

· ·

I'm sure you'll find teaching through multimedia more rewarding for you and your students than teaching without multimedia. And I can almost guarantee that the knowledge gained through the creation of multimedia masterpieces will stay in their heads longer than any boring old lecture or filmstrip.

The Activities

I've divided these activities by subject area, and I've purposely left off grade-level assignments. As teachers, we quickly learn to alter activities to meet our needs. So scale things down or beef them up to fit your own individual needs.

The activities can be created with just about any of the multimedia composition programs mentioned in this book. However, *HyperStudio* or *HyperCard* will provide the interactive aspect of buttons that link information. If you teach early elementary students, you will probably want to use *KidPix2, Multimedia Workshop, KidPix Studio,* or *Monstrous Media Kid.* These programs don't allow you to link information with buttons on each card; however, you can create slide shows that take the viewer through a presentation in an order that you predetermine.

Note: If you or your students are not familiar with the terms *buttons, stacks, cards,* or any of the others used in describing these activities, please review the software mentioned in Chapters 8 through 11 (or take a look at Appendix A).

Language Arts

The possibilities for multimedia in the area of language arts are endless. See what you think about my ideas and then come up with some of your own.

Technical writing

This area is one of those skills that the tests keep telling us the students need to master. Why not let your students have a little fun while practicing the skill — and wind up with a neat presentation to boot?

These stacks could start and end with cards showing the ultimate goal or finished product. The other cards could each feature a step involved in the process. The cards could include video footage, text, audio, drawings, photos, or a combination of any of these media. Following are a few projects that I think would work great with the technical writing goal:

- ✔ **Electronic Recipe Books:** You might have each child bring in a favorite recipe and create cards that give step-by-step directions on preparing the food. Then compile all the cards for a great Mother's Day present.

- ✔ **Favorite Art Projects:** As the year progresses, why not create a presentation on each art project that your class creates? This activity would provide a visual reference for your students next year — and it will keep you up-to-date on what you've done in the past.

- ✔ **Create Your Own Game:** My students love this one. Allow groups of students to create their own computer game. The buttons placed on the cards could be designed to elicit specific responses. (If the students answer a question incorrectly, the next card reveals a prison or dungeon, while a correct response leads them further into the game.)

- ✔ **Sega or Nintendo Game Tips:** I don't care how children practice their writing skills as long as they're writing! Topics of interest make students feel like *instant experts*. I can't tell you how often I've heard video game tricks being discussed in my classroom. Why not set your students to work creating stacks of cards to enlighten the masses?

Choose-your-own-ending stories

Kids love those mystery/adventure books that allow the reader to decide on the course of action. (You know: Turn to page 25 if Jane should run after the burglar. Turn to page 40 if you think that she should go into the old house.) Through the use of an interactive multimedia authoring program such as

HyperStudio, buttons on cards can act like the little make-a-choice phrases in the books. You'll be surprised at how creative and involved your students' stories might become! The addition of sound effects, movies, and animation works in well with this project also.

Persuasive writing

Assign students the task of convincing you (the mayor) to add a business to the city. They can decide whether the new business is to be an amusement park, a zoo, an arcade, or whatever they like. Then through a multimedia presentation, they must prove that this new business would be "a good thing" for the city.

Creative writing

E-books: Programs such as *HyperStudio* and *HyperCard* allow you to create invisible buttons on a card. These buttons can take on a variety of actions, such as animation, sounds, or movies. This control can help students create their own version of *e-books* (electronic books) similar to those produced by Brøderbund (see the demonstration on the *Mac Multimedia For Teachers CD*). Only this time, the e-books are based around the students' own creative story pursuits.

Open-ended stories: I love doing this project throughout the year. Open-ended stories are my version of multimedia Mad Libs. Have students in one class begin a story in a multimedia program and then exchange their story for one created by another class. Have the other class finish your students' story while your class finishes the other group's story. Be sure to add in all types of multimedia elements. This activity also works great with long-distance learning arrangements and online pen pals.

Class magazines

Class magazines could be done on a monthly or quarterly basis. The magazine's pages could include audio or video clips of students reading their articles. Involve those students who are more artistically inclined to contribute artwork, photos, and layout design. Buttons on pages might take viewers to a card with biographical information about each author.

Write a multimedia resume

Direct your students to sell themselves and their qualities. Have each student create a four-card stack highlighting their special strengths and qualities. Include a video clip to demonstrate the qualities, and maybe include a little snappy audio clip to convince the viewers that they'd be right for the job.

Create a multimedia catalog

Have your students do a little dreaming and create their own wishbook for Christmas. Students could write advertising copy for the item they most want to see under their tree on Christmas morning. Compile all of the items into a catalog that talks, has video demonstrations of the products, has incredible drawings, and includes a few digital pictures.

Parts of speech or punctuation

By programming buttons, you can create your own skill-and-drill-type stack. You might have a sentence on each page that either has a word underlined or punctuation missing. Three buttons at the bottom of the page could have possible answers. Two of the buttons would contain incorrect answers and, when clicked, would be programmed to take the user to a "Sorry, Wrong Answer" card. The correct response might take the user to a card with the completed sentence and a congratulatory message. This activity could be adapted for many different grade and skill levels.

Math

Math multimedia presentations work great for students who need enrichment in math — you know the kids I'm talking about: You give them a sheet of 100 problems, and they've finished before you've gotten back to your seat.

Flash cards

Many teachers in my school create presentations that contain basic facts (addition, subtraction, multiplication, and division). They'll make one card showing a problem and the next card containing its answer. By timing how long the card stays on the screen, this setup doesn't even require buttons. The teachers then play the presentation as a loop (which keeps repeating over and over again) in the morning or whenever the computer isn't in use, and the presentation serves as a constant skill-and-drill.

Critical thinking and problem solving

Critical thinking and problem solving are other areas of concern each year when standardized test scores are published. Why not find a good set of problems and assign students the task of illustrating these problems through the use of multimedia?

Johnny needs $12 to buy a ticket to the concert. How many glasses of lemonade will he have to sell in order to clear this much profit? Lemons cost. . . .

You get the picture. They would be learning as they plot out each card in this fun stack. (Wow! I guess planning these involved presentations requires quite a bit of critical thinking itself!)

Polls and graphs

Kids love to wander the halls of the school and conduct surveys. After compiling their data, have your students keep an ongoing presentation of their survey results throughout the year in the form of a multimedia presentation. Persuasion software does a great job of converting data into cool graphs or charts. Your class might even throw in some live video footage of students taking the polls or audio clips of the questions being answered.

Social Studies

I've found social studies to be one of the easiest areas of the curriculum to teach through multimedia. See if you find these activities exciting enough to change the way you teach social studies.

Welcome Wagon

Community awareness is the goal here. Have the students research events, tourist attractions, goods, and services in your hometown. Then compile this knowledge to create a multimedia presentation that could be on display in City Hall to welcome and inform newcomers and visitors. Try to incorporate as much freedom and interactivity as possible within the cards to allow all users to customize the presentation to meet their specific needs.

Biographical sketches

The *TIME Magazine* CD does a great job with biographical data. Have your students look at this CD and then branch out on their own and create their own multimedia biography of a person in the past or present. Interactive elements throughout the stack could allow the viewer to jump to different time periods and events in the person's life.

Tip: If your students can't find actual film footage, why not have them reenact the period of time or event in history, record it onto videotape, and then save the videotape as a QuickTime movie?

Instructional presentations

This stack could take the viewer through a process or event, such as how a bill becomes a law, daily life in colonial Jamestown, travel with the Lewis and Clark expedition, and so forth. The purpose of a stack such as this would be to enlighten and inform the viewer about a specific event or time period. A main screen might connect the viewer to different aspects of the subject rather than simply go through the information in a linear manner.

Historical "What if . . . "

This project is tons of fun. Give your students a historical twist: What if the British empire still governed the American colonies? Then encourage them to create a presentation based around this supposition. Make sure that they base their assumptions on actual historical facts.

Family tree

Expensive genealogy programs that compile all the information for you are on the market — but where's the challenge in that? This project would be a great gift for a grandparent. It would be a good idea to have your students include scanned-in photos, newspaper clippings, video clips, and background music from the time period of each person's life.

Olympic venue

Living in Atlanta, I'm very proud of the fact that the International Olympic Committee found my hometown worthy enough to host the 1996 games. Give your students the task of convincing the Olympic Committee to allow your city to host the games.

Architectural review board

Take your students and a digital camera on a tour of your town and take pictures of all the interesting buildings that you see. When you get back, have the students create an informative presentation on the amazing architectural finds within your own community.

Science

Science is all about documentation of facts. Hopefully, the activities in this section will help students document their studies in an interesting way.

Step-by-step science experiments

Have students create science experiment stacks that are open-ended and contain areas for students to record their own hypotheses, data, and experiment results. These stacks could be saved and then compiled to show whole-class data.

Inventions

Each group of two or three students could be assigned the task of creating an invention that uses a scientific principle currently being studied in class. Each step of the invention process could be documented with digital photos and audio narration. The final card might include a video of the invention at work.

The legal stuff

Please make sure that the media clips (graphics, movies, photos, text, animation) you use within your presentations are either royalty-free or are personal creations of you or your students. Copyright infringement is a major concern within the computer and publishing industries.

Also note the fine print. Although many of the media clips may claim to be royalty-free, many do require compensation if the end product is to be used in a profitmaking venture.

Environmental concerns

Multimedia presentations featuring environmental concerns are being created on a daily basis by environmental groups around the world. The purpose of the presentations is to inform and enlighten. Challenge your students to take up an environmental cause and convince the rest of the class that their cause is worthy of concern.

Health

Health is probably one of the hardest subjects to fit into your daily schedule. I hope these activities will help you and your children find time for this important subject.

Systems of the body

This presentation has great potential. You might start out with an overview of a human body cutaway (you know, like those we used to see in our old biology books) and then have buttons that take viewers to separate stacks on the different body systems.

Health concerns instructional stacks

There's a myriad of concerns and troubles facing today's children that we could have never imagined when we were kids. So the more ways you can get a message across, the better. Why not have older students create interactive stacks on health issues, such as drug use, nutrition, AIDS, dental hygiene, and personal safety.

Miscellaneous

Here are a few more ideas that didn't seem to fit into the normal curriculum channels.

Class yearbook

The possibilities are endless here. The yearbook could be as simple as an opening page (maybe a class picture) and a card for each student. Or it could be as elaborate as an opening movie, a card for each student (including a video or photo CD image and maybe even a taped statement), inserted cards that cover events throughout the year, and maybe a few interviews with the teachers, the principal, and other significant school personnel.

Class timeline

I've done this activity with a simple word-processing program. I had one student enter the highlights of the preceding week and then compiled the journal entries into one big class timeline at the end of the year. Multimedia software allows you to step things up a notch or two by including graphics, movies, or sound with each week's entry.

Field trip highlights

Digital cameras were tailor-made for this project. The next time you take your students on a field trip, don't forget your digital camera (Apple QuickTake, Canon Xap, Kodak DC 40) and your video camera. When you return, have your students create a cool presentation about your trip.

Contest clues

If you are planning to enter your students' productions in any type of multimedia competition, you should know that the main ingredients judges look for are originality and student-created work. That means that the judges don't want you to retell the same old Pilgrim story, and they don't want to see tons of store-bought clip art or movies.

If you choose a common topic, such as the Pilgrims, put a different slant on it. Tell your viewers something they might not have known, or tell the story from a completely different perspective. You're going for the "Wow, that's original!" response.

And by all means, don't use those tired old *KidPix* stamps. We've all seen them a million times. Judges love original artwork. The same thing goes for video footage or photos. It's easy to order a disk of clip art. True talent and creativity show up only when students take the time to create the work themselves.

The beauty of a multimedia project isn't seen in the end result as some may think. It's the learning that goes on during the creation of the project that should get all the attention and glory.

Write to me on America Online (MNette) and share your experiences (good and bad). I'd love to hear about your multimedia-curriculum integration.

Top Ten Multimedia Presentation Tips

1. Try to be consistent with fonts. The use of more than two or three fonts in a presentation can confuse viewers. Along the same lines, be constant with the fonts you choose for titles and body text.

2. Keep words and phrases short. This is one time in education when incomplete sentences are welcomed.

3. Don't forget what you are trying to portray. All too often students get excited by the potential of multimedia and stray away from the intended purpose — what the presentation is about gets lost in a sea of flashy graphics, QuickTime movies, and confusing transitions.

4. Keep backgrounds consistent for a professional look and feel.

5. Place buttons in a consistent spot. Many of the presentation programs allow you to create invisible buttons, and students find these buttons fun to create. However, it's hard for someone else to guess where the buttons may be hidden.

6. Be sure to include a button on each slide of a presentation to allow the viewer the option of exiting the program at any point.

7. Keep sounds consistent and as close to the theme of the presentation as possible. Students like the sound a monkey makes; however, this sound doesn't really belong in a presentation on the Renaissance!

8. Transitions between slides should be smooth and not take away from the flow of the presentation. Sometimes it works best to stick with one type of transition for the entire presentation.

9. Use borders around graphics and photos to make them stand out from their backgrounds.

10. People always remember the beginning and the end of a presentation. That's why lawyers give those glorious opening statements and fiery closing arguments. Think like a lawyer — wow the audience with your presentation's opening, and leave the audience speechless (except for compliments) with your presentation's closing!

Part IV
Sharing with Others

The 5th Wave
By Rich Tennant

"IT WAS BETWEEN THAT AND NEW CLASSROOM COMPUTERS."

In this part . . .

*1*deal with the concept of sharing on a daily basis — living with a two-year-old and a four-year-old forces me to deal with the issue.

Teachers who are willing to share their successes and failures are wonderful jewels. In education, I think I've learned more from other teachers than I did in graduate school. You need to learn from others who are experiencing your situation.

Multimedia is a broad topic that appeals to many. In this part, I'll show you ways to save your productions and make them portable. So go ahead: take your productions on the road and inform the masses. I can almost guarantee that you'll learn something along the way, too.

Chapter 13
Taking Your Show on the Road

. . . .

In This Chapter
▶ Storage solutions simplified
▶ DDDD (Distinctive differences in drives demystified)
▶ Tape back-up explained
▶ Compression software conquered

. . . .

I've mentioned before that multimedia presentations take up mega amounts of space on your hard drive. This fact hit home in a big way early in my multimedia pursuits after a group of third-grade students had worked for weeks on a wonderful project that they planned to enter in the county media festival.

The presentation was superb. I knew it was destined to be a winner. However, when it came time for me to send it in for judging, the presentation was far too large to fit onto even a high-density disk. It was the day before the entry was due, and I couldn't get it off my hard-drive! This outstanding multimedia presentation ran beautifully from my computer, but I couldn't pack up my computer and set it up for the judges. I had to maintain my *teacher facade* for the students and pretend that I knew what I was doing. I assured them that I'd get their presentation to the competition and then took a crash course on alternative storage methods.

Well, this chapter will help you avoid an eleventh-hour disaster like mine. (By the way, the presentation did eventually make it to the local competition and has gone on to international competition.)

The Dilemma

Your computer's hard drive has a limited space and can therefore hold only a limited amount of information; and as your skills and interest in multimedia grow, you'll soon fill that space and begin begging for more. This is what I like to call a *good problem*. You need more space because you've decided to really put your computer and your talent to work.

When you reach this memory-saturation point, you and your administrators need to start thinking about allocating money for alternative storage space. External storage devices are quickly becoming standard issue in schools today, and the variety of choices can sometimes be mind-boggling.

Stuff to Think About

Three major considerations apply to all the different types of external storage devices:

- ✔ how fast they are (speed)
- ✔ how much *stuff* they can hold (capacity)
- ✔ whether they are standard external hard drives (with a fixed capacity), removable cartridge drives, or tape backup systems

Speed

Speed refers to how much time it takes the hard drive to access your information. This time is measured in milliseconds. The lower the access time, the better. Most of today's drives have access times that range between 8 and 15 milliseconds.

Speed is not very important when you're putting together your multimedia presentations. Sure, it's a hassle to wait a few extra seconds while your computer pulls up that color graphic, but the graphic gets there eventually. However, speed becomes critically important when you're playing back your multimedia creations. If the viewer has to wait even a few extra seconds between transitions, the effect of a presentation can be totally lost.

Capacity

Capacity refers to the amount of information measured in *megabytes (MB)* — and now *gigabytes (GB)* — that your hard drive has room for. I recommend that you start out with at least 300MB of space when you purchase an external hard drive. Remember that every facet of multimedia requires major amounts of memory — a second of QuickTime footage can possibly eat up about 30K of storage space.

Open your wallet wide and spend it all! That's right: Buy the biggest hard drive you can afford. Otherwise you'll be buying more space again before you know it.

Type

I'm sure that you're tired of making choices (or at least thinking about having to make choices) at this point. But guess what? I've got one more choice for you to make. In the world of external hard drives, you need to consider two basic breeds when you're thinking about multimedia sharing: external hard drives and removable drives.

External hard drives, cartridge drives, and tape back-up systems connect to your computer via the *SCSI* (Small Computer System Interface) *port* on the back of your computer. When you've got one of these additional units hooked up to your Mac, the additional unit's icon will appear just below your Mac's hard-drive icon on your screen. Double-clicking the additional unit's icon will open it and show the add-on's contents just like Mac's hard-drive icon reveals what's in your computer's built-in drive.

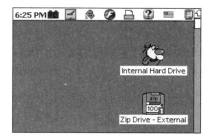

External hard drives

External hard drives were your only choice for additional storage in the beginning. They were very popular, mainly because they were first on the scene. However, external hard drives have a fixed amount of space available; and once that space is filled, you'll need to buy another hard drive.

One bonus to having an external hard drive is that Apple-compatible external hard drives are automatically recognized by Macs. That is, no special software is needed if you take your external drive to another school and use its computer to show off your creations.

I think that some people feel more comfortable with these drives because they think that all their information is safely tucked away on a disk they can't see inside the hard plastic box that contains their external hard drive. They don't want to think about their information being on little disks that pop in and out of the drive as in the next example.

External hard drives can cost anywhere from $300 for a 270MB drive all the way up to $1,500 for a 2GB drive.

Removable cartridge drives

These babies work just like external hard drives, except your storage capacity is *almost* unlimited with removable drives. (*Almost* means that you're only limited by the amount of space on each cartridge.) You see, with removable drives, your information is stored on cartridges that you put into and take out of the drive.

The size of the cartridges varies based on the type of drive you purchase. But the cool part is, you only have to buy *one* drive — it never fills up; you just keep buying additional cartridges.

If it's necessary, a removable drive comes with the required software. You'll have to load this software to enable your computer to understand that you've attached a little friend. (This really isn't a big deal.)

<u>SyQuest and Bernoulli drives</u>

SyQuest and Bernoulli drives are the most popular removable drives on the market. They look and function in similar ways. SyQuest drives can read only SyQuest cartridges. Bernoulli drives can read only Bernoulli cartridges.

The drives are formatted to read a certain size of cartridge; they can usually read a smaller size of cartridge than they are formatted for, but they can never read a larger size of cartridge. My advice is to buy a drive that will read the largest cartridges — right now the largest cartridges are 270MB.

SyQuest removable drives are the most popular of the two and will cost anywhere between $300 and $500. SyQuest cartridges cost between $60 and $80 based on the amount of information they can hold. Bernoulli drives cost about the same, but their cartridges are a bit more pricey, between $95 and $110.

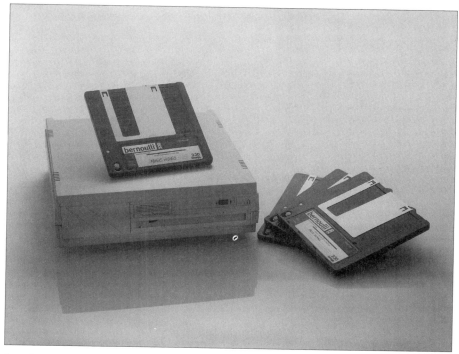

Bernoulli drive (photo courtesy of Iomega Corp.)

Iomega Zip drive

The Iomega Zip drive is a little different from either the SyQuest or the Bernoulli drive. On the Zip drive, all your information is stored on a little 100MB disk that's not much bigger than your standard floppy disk. However, unlike the SyQuest or Bernoulli drives that have their read-write mechanisms within the cartridge you insert, the guts (the read-write mechanism) of this guy are inside the drive itself.

Zip drive (photo courtesy of Iomega Corp.)

This drive is significantly cheaper than the SyQuest and Bernoulli drives, and schools are scooping them up! Another bonus is the size (significantly smaller than your average textbook). This smallness makes it very easy to slide the drive into your book bag or briefcase and take along.

At the time of this printing, a Zip drive was going for about $200 and came with one 100MB disk. Additional 100MB disks listed at about $20. Rumor has it that Iomega is coming out with a new drive called the JAZ drive. It will be a little more costly, but it will work with 1GB disks. Wow!

Tape Backup Systems

Tape backup systems are sometimes referred to as *DAT systems* in catalogs. This new acronym stands for *digital audio tape*. They're great for storing large amounts of information in an archival manner. (*Archived information* is information that you won't need to access on a daily basis.) You see, a tape system reads and writes information in a linear manner and can move only forward or backward to access your information — this process can take a considerable amount of time. However, your disk drives have little arms that can move over the disk at will to locate information in a much more timely fashion, as shown in the following diagram.

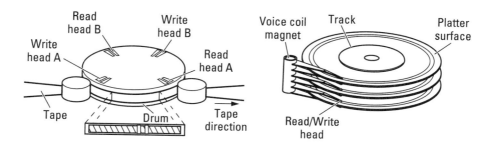

On the plus side, tape backup systems are very cost efficient, an important factor in the world of public education. Drives start at about $600, and the tapes only run between $7 and $20, depending on the amount of information they can hold.

On the downside, the tapes are easily corrupted. After all, they look and function just like the cassettes you keep in your listening center, and how many of those cassettes have you either rewound with the eraser end of a pencil or simply thrown away because they've lost their sound quality?

Compression Software

For those of us on a very limited budget (myself included), there's still one other alternative: compression software. Compression software isn't a good long-term alternative for major multimedia production, but it'll get you out of a jam every now and then.

Compression software allows you to "stuff" large files into smaller documents called archives. These archives are much smaller than the original documents, so compression makes documents easier to fit on a disk, quicker to send through your modem, and faster to backup. Really big files can sometimes be broken up into smaller stuffed archives and then rejoined later.

After a presentation has been stuffed and transferred to another location, the presentation needs to be unstuffed (and, in larger cases, rejoined) in order to be fully functional. That requires the new location to have the same software program in order to unstuff your document, which can be a drawback.

An alternative solution to this dilemma is to create something called a *self-extracting archive (SEA)*. You can create an SEA with a program called *Stuffit Deluxe*. The command to make an SEA appears in a menu bar. SEAs encode your stuffed files with the software necessary to unstuff the files the first time you open them.

This system works out great if you're sharing files with friends in other locations (long-distance learning-sharing arrangements).

Take a look at the shareware compression program *Stuffit Lite* that's on the *Mac Multimedia For Teachers* CD.

Confused?

I hope these explanations have enlightened and not bewildered you. In any case, I think that I've exposed you to a variety of good storage and retrieval options. I also want you to know that every school in America isn't fortunate enough to have the funds needed to make these purchases — don't feel neglected.

In the next chapter, I'll discuss some of the ways and places you can show off after you've made your creations portable. I'll also review the process for dumping your presentation to a videotape.

Now that I've got this great external storage space . . .

You treat new students in your classroom just as you treat the others. Well, the same is true for this new member of your desktop — treat your new storage space the same as you treat your original hard drive. It's a simple case of drag and drop. Just as you'd drag something to your hard drive for storage or even to a specific folder on your hard drive, do the same with your new little friend.

When choosing to save a document you're working on, click the Desktop button and then double-click your new storage device. It's simple!

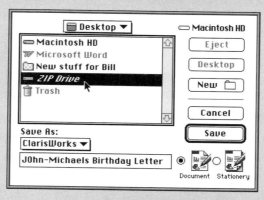

Chapter 14

Showing Off

• •

In This Chapter

▶ Showing off can be a good thing
▶ The best spots to show off

• •

*P*olo men's cologne smells great. It certainly gets my attention when my husband decides to splash a little on — builders rarely smell like designer fragrances. That's why I immediately recognized the cologne one Monday morning as the scent overcame me and the rest of my class. You see, Ryan, the smallest child in the third grade, had been given a bottle of Polo cologne for his birthday (I know: a rather strange gift for an eight-year-old). By choosing to show off his new present on that Monday morning in my classroom, little Ryan gained the attention he'd always longed for — every girl in the class wanted to be near him.

The next morning, I could immediately tell that Ryan's showing off had paid off for him — each and every boy in my class had decided to splash on a little of his dad's cologne before coming to school! (It wasn't hard for me to discern the Old Spice dads from the Aramis dads.) Although my classroom smelled like the men's fragrance counter at Neiman Marcus, Ryan was riding high with pride and attention.

Whether you want to admit it or not, showing off gets attention. And a little attention goes a long way when it comes to persuading others to follow suit.

In this chapter, I'll show you some ways in which you can make the art of showing off work for you — and I promise that none my methods involve the sense of smell. Keeping others aware of your technological success is important in order to justify increased spending on all the *little extras* you need to make the most of multimedia.

So, why do you want an AV Mac?

This is a question administrators may very well ask when you excitedly tell them you've *got* to have an AV machine. An AV Mac is a costly addition for any school to consider, so make sure that it's something you really need before getting on your hands and knees begging your principal or PTA to write a check.

Let's first examine what you'll get with an AV Mac. You'll be able to import live video or video previously shot via your VCR or video camera. You'll also be able to export anything on your computer screen to a televison for recording to video tape — or maybe you just want what's on your computer to appear on a large screen TV for presentations. If you're interested in doing everything I've just mentioned, you need to purchase an AV Mac.

But hey, maybe all you want to be able to do is get your kids' presentations onto video tape so that these presentations can be shown to parents at home or on your school's closed circuit television system. If that's the case, or if you just want what's on your screen to appear on a larger monitor or televison, you'll do just fine if you purchase a presentation system like the Apple Presentation System mentioned in this chapter. It's a cheaper alternative (around $260), and you may already have a computer that will support the system.

If importing shots you've taken with your video camera is your goal, you may want to go with the purchase of a package like *VideoSpigot* that, when installed, enables you to import video and manipulate your footage on the computer screen. You can use this video footage later in your multimedia presentations.

How to Show Off

I hope you've read Chapter 13 and have some good ideas about meeting your external storage needs and making your presentations more portable. I pity the poor souls I see at conferences transporting their entire computer setup because they don't have a viable alternative — desktop computers should stay on your desktop.

Apple Presentation System

This system will allow you to connect your computer to a television (make that a big-screen TV, if possible) for giving presentations to large groups, or you can use this setup when doing whole-class computer instruction. What you see on your computer screen will also appear on the television screen. You control things from your keyboard while the audience sees and hears what's happening on the TV screen.

The Apple Presentation System consists of a video conversion box, a DB-15 cable to connect the conversion box to your computer, and S-video composite cables for connection with the TV's Video In port. (**Note:** If you'll be using this system with any of the one-piece Macs, such as the 550, 575, 580, or 5200 models, you'll also have to purchase a $45 adapter for the monitor. The 550 and 575 require a third-party add-on that is different from what Apple sells for the 580 and 5200) The Apple Presentation System is very easy to set up, and you can get all this for the low educational price of about $260 if you're one of the first 100 callers! (Just kidding. Any educator can get it for that price; off the shelf, it's about $100 more than that.)

This system is the way to go if you want to put your presentations on videotape and don't have an AV Mac. If you've got a VCR hooked up to the TV that you're using for display, just pop in a tape and press that record button.

Please note that this system *doesn't replace* the capabilities you get with an AV Mac. The Apple Presentation System only enables you to export your media to another source; it doesn't let you import video footage.

Other computer-to-television adapters

Other companies also make computer-to-TV adapters that will work with your Mac. At this time, however, most of those adapters don't transfer your sound along with the visual image. That means you'll probably need a good set of speakers attached to your Mac in order to have good audio quality for your presentation.

On the other hand, these converters do offer some other bonuses, such as remote controls that enable you to click from a distance or zoom in on a particular area of the screen (my husband could go pro as remote-control clicker if remote-control clicking ever becomes an Olympic event). Many of the units are also compatible with the *Electronic Marker* software (see the sidebar "You can have John Madden's job" for a description of this software). Many of these converters are also cross-platform units (that is, they'll work with Apple as well as IBM-compatible machines). Two sources for this software that I recommend are Focus Enhancements (617-938-8088) and Consumer Technology Northwest (503-643-1662). The converters can be purchased for $250 – $400.

(photo courtesy of Consumer Technology Northwest, Inc.)

LCD panels

LCD panels for the Mac have been around for a while now. An *LCD panel* is a device that you connect to your computer's monitor port by using the cable that's provided with your LCD panel. You then place the LCD panel on top of an overhead projector's transparency table. This setup allows you to see what's on the computer in a larger format than you can project onto a movie screen. Most of the newer models enable you to see the image both on your computer screen and on the movie screen onto which you are projecting the image via the overhead projector. When LCD panels were introduced, the images weren't all that clear, and colors appeared to be washed out on the screen. However, the technology has greatly improved, and you see LCD panels in use for presentations everywhere (but to get a sharp picture, you need a very bright overhead projector). Most LCD panels start at about $1,000 and can go much higher.

Read the fine print and ask questions before you make your purchase. Some LCD panels will work with IBM-compatible machines (and those antiquated Apple IIs) as well as Macs. Remote controls that enable you to click forward in a slide show when you're not standing at the computer are often part of bundled packages.

Smart View 3600 (photo courtesy of In Focus Systems)

You can have John Madden's job

This little software package is really great. *Electronic Marker* (Consumer Technology Northwest, 503-643-1662, $24) turns your cursor into a marker and enables you to mark up your screen just like the announcers do on *Monday Night Football*. By simply moving your mouse, you can draw on top of your screen image without altering the original work. This function is great for emphasizing points or highlighting examples during large-group presentations.

Please touch!

Edmark has created a nifty little device called the TouchWindow. TouchWindows work great for presentations in school settings. The window enables viewers simply to touch the screen instead of clicking the mouse to access information or participate in multimedia presentations. The TouchWindow costs $300 and comes with all the necessary software and cables.

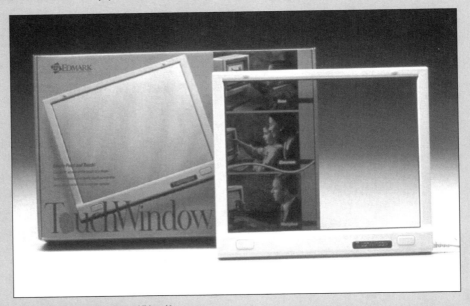

TouchWindow (photo courtesy of Edmark)

Dumping to video

If you can't manage to get your presentation on some type of external storage device in order to run the presentation on a larger screen, another option is dumping it to video. *Dumping to video* simply means connecting your computer to your TV/VCR (making what's on your monitor appear on your TV screen) and actually recording what you do on the computer to videotape. In order to do this, you'll need an AV Mac or a conversion package, such as the Apple Presentation System.

Radio Shack to the rescue!

I'm embarassed to say this, but up until a few years ago, you couldn't have paid me to shop at a Radio Shack. It might sound silly, but I saw that store as the ultimate nerd hangout — not that I'm some totally cool being. However, I've had to eat my words, and I now view the store and its employees in a different light.

Multimedia in education can prove to be frustrating when it comes to cables. I'm constantly in need of an extra cable, an adaptor for the end of my cable, or a longer cable. Most schools have a virtual potpourri of computer models, audio equipment, and video equipment; and our not-so-nerdy friends at Radio Shack have the cables and adaptors that will work with most models.

I've already covered using the Apple Presentation System to get your multi-media presentations onto a video monitor. The following directions explain how to use your AV Mac to get your presentations onto videotape. Make sure that you're working on an AV Mac or a Mac that has an AV card installed. If you have an AV card installed, the back of your computer may look a little different, but the ports are the same.

1. Use an S-video cable (or the yellow part of an RCA jack) to connect the AV Mac's Video Out to your VCR's Video In. (Power Macs come with an output adapter.)

2. Next you'll need to use a dual phono cable to connect the Mac's speaker jack with the VCR's Audio In jack or jacks.

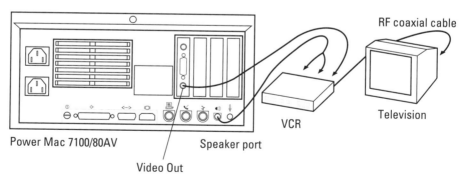

Power Mac 7100/80AV

Video Out

Speaker port

VCR

RF coaxial cable

Television

3. Now open your System Folder (on your hard drive); then open the Control Panels folder. Double-click the Monitors control panel and make sure that the number of colors is set for the same number that it was when you created your project.

This setting is especially significant if you created your project on another machine that may have been set to a different number of colors.

4. Next click the Options button.

5. Click the button labeled Display Video on Television. A new screen greets you and awaits your commands.

In the Monitor Type list, choose the correct resolution for your Mac. Choose 640 × 480 pixels to ensure that you'll get the entire image when recording. You should also check the Flicker-Free Format box to ensure that you'll get the best possible image.

Note: Never select the Upon Restart Display Video on Television checkbox. If you lose your video signal, you'll be in big trouble when you restart the computer and are greeted with a blank monitor and a blank TV screen.

6. Click OK. A dialog box appears and asks whether you're sure that you want to display your screen on the television.

   This is a good time to check your cable connections, make sure that you've rewound that videotape, and take a sip of coffee.

   Click OK and, after a few seconds, your monitor will go black — and you should see your screen image appear on the TV. I've been told that some of the new Mac models enable you to view your image on both the computer monitor *and* the television, much like you can with the Apple Presentation System.

7. Now you're ready to record. Get your presentation up on the screen and ready to go.

   When all is set, push that record button and do your thing. If you are clicking through the presentation as you record, be sure to leave enough time for viewers to read any text or take in details of the graphic elements.

8. After you finish, you'll need to go back to that same Monitors control panel and switch back to the computer monitor.

Like just about everything in life (such as getting the first lunch period or the last recess time slot), there are advantages and disadvantages to dumping your creations onto videotape.

Pros of video dumping

✔ Dumping to video allows you to make a copy of presentations. Students can take the videotaped copies home and show them to their parents. Just about everyone has access to a VCR, although a Mac in the home may not be commonplace yet.

TV/VCR combination units

For about $300 you can purchase a compact little TV/VCR combination unit that really comes in handy when it comes time to transfer your creations to videotape. These combo units are great space savers for the multimedia-computing teachers who (more than likely) already have a scanner, color printer, external hard drive, modem, CD-ROM drive, and speakers on their desks. I keep my TV/VCR unit right beside my computer so that it's easy to access the cables and ports when I'm ready to transfer a new masterpiece to videotape.

✔ You won't have to worry about playback problems if you did a good job recording the presentation to tape. There won't be snags if you went through the interactive portions of the program before you taped and made sure to leave plenty of time for viewers to experience the screen before moving on to the next portion of your presentation.

✔ Dumping to videotape is a great way to share your presentations with others in the school via closed-circuit television.

Cons of video dumping

✔ The biggest disadvantage has to be the loss of all interactive elements. The most exciting aspects of multimedia presentations are the interactive elements (click here to hear a sound, click here to watch the movie, and so forth). We all love control, and that element is gone when someone else does the clicking for you in order to record to videotape.

✔ You lose a great deal of screen clarity and color variations. A computer monitor has a much better picture than any television can provide.

✔ After the presentation is on videotape, you can't go back and change anything without recording it again. So be sure that you save your computer version of the presentation on your hard disk or some other type of external storage device.

Where to Show Off

Well, now that you know *how* to show off, let's discuss *where* you can show off. I'm not talking about the teachers' lounge, where you might be found bragging about the fact that the superintendent's daughter didn't end up in your class this year or that you've managed to avoid having car duty on each of the past five rainy days. No, this showing off will feature your students' work and, hopefully, at the same time, shine the spotlight on you and the wonders of technology in the school setting.

Media festivals

There are a number of media festivals across the country that are wonderful outlets for showing off your students' accomplishments. The most well known of these is the International Media Festival. The competition starts at the local school level and goes on to full-fledged international competition. I've learned so much about multimedia as a judge at these festivals, and the kids love the public recognition of their accomplishments. Your media specialist should be able to put you in touch with the proper people.

America Online

When sending your presentations online, be prepared to use a good chunk of your precious online time for uploading these memory-intensive creations.

- ✔ Hook up with another teacher who's using *HyperStudio, KidPix Studio, Multimedia Workshop,* or any of the other great presentation titles, and make an arrangement to share stacks or slide shows.
- ✔ Go to keyword **HyperStudio** and upload your stacks for the folks at Roger Wagner Publishing (and anyone else who's interested) to enjoy.

PTA

The PTA folks need to stay informed of your technology pursuits. Keeping them informed is the best method that I've found to encourage them to donate matching funds to keep our technology up to date. One of the best ways to keep the PTA informed is to have a brief student-created presentation ready to show just before each general PTA meeting and each executive officers' meeting. I have the children who created the presentation run things and answer questions afterwards. These presentations never fail to wow the PTA crowd.

Professional conferences

Take your show on the road. That's right. Find out about conferences being held in your area and go spread the word. Don't worry about whether or not what you've done with multimedia will be interesting to someone else. There's always someone who's just starting out, and there's always someone who wants to learn more; both will be interested in what you and your students have been up to.

Often the conferences allow free admission to anyone who's willing to present at a session. So go for it. Speaking at a session takes only an hour or two of your time, and the rest of the conference will be all yours.

Have a dry run-through before you present

Remember when we were student teaching and knew that we were going to be observed the next day? Gosh! I'd time my lesson, rehearse in front of a mirror, and even pretend that my poor cat was a student (thanks, Chelsea!).

Well, in a more subdued manner, that's what you need to do before giving a multimedia presen-tation, especially if you've taken your show on the road and are using unfamiliar equipment. Get there an hour or two early and try everything out. Work out all the kinks *before* the curtain goes up and the spotlight's beaming down onto your monitor.

Teacher inservices

There is no better way to get teachers excited about a project than by telling and showing them what great feats their peers are accomplishing. Do an in-service on *HyperStudio* (or any of the other presentation software programs) and let teachers who are already using aspects of multimedia be the stars for a day. Have them show off their accomplishments, and I can almost guarantee that the school's interest level in multimedia will grow at a rapid pace.

Technology Week activities

Technology Week usually falls in early February. This is a great time to highlight what you and your students have accomplished by using multimedia. Have a technology open house where you highlight different areas of technology and show how your school is using technology in the educational setting.

Cable television

Many local cable television companies are more than willing to highlight student work on their public access channels. Contact your local cable com-pany and see about setting up a monthly or quarterly time slot to run multime-dia presentations created by the students from your school.

Closed-circuit television

Most new schools are being equipped with closed-circuit television. *Closed-circuit* simply means that all the classroom televisions are wired together and can access the same information on one channel that is broadcast from a specific location (usually the media center). If your school has closed-circuit capabilities, you can play one video, and each television in the school can watch it; or even better, you can broadcast your own morning or afternoon news programs.

At my school, we have a morning news crew that handles all the announcements (live, on the air) for the first ten minutes of each school day. We also use this time slot to show off any newly created multimedia presentations.

Now that you're well versed on creating vivacious video, sampling sensational sounds, and grabbing grandiose graphics, go out and wow the masses.

Practice makes perfect

Be sure to run through your presentation before you begin dumping to the video. This step will save you immeasurable amounts of time and frustration. (Many a time I've been in a hurry to get something on tape and was not really sure that I knew the proper sequence of events.) You want the presentation to flow in a smooth path — not knowing what button to click or hesitating before starting a QuickTime movie might cause your viewer to lose interest.

Part V
The Part of Tens

In this part . . .

1've been told that this part is a tradition with IDG Books Worldwide. And, being the superstitious person that I am, I still worry about the fact that I failed to include this section in my first book (an oversight that I'll be sure to remedy in the second edition).

Anyway, in this part you'll find lists and brief descriptions of programs that I personally feel are the best when it comes to multimedia. Highlight the ones you like and call MacWarehouse — the programs will be on your doorstep the next morning.

I highlight the best interactive-learning CDs in lists broken down by grade level. You'll also find lists of great multimedia authoring programs as well as sound-effect, video-clip, and graphics-collection CDs that help you add that extra pizzazz needed to keep kids interested in learning.

Chapter 15

Top Ten (Well, Maybe More than Ten) Interactive-Learning CDs

· ·

*N*ot all CDs are created equal. This is a truism that you will soon discover if you make your purchases based on packaging claims or slick advertising. I've been taken in by these ploys more often than I care to admit. Read reviews, talk to other teachers, and seek out demo versions of CDs whenever possible. Know this, too: An exceptional item in print doesn't always get translated into a superb example on CD. The lists in this chapter present my personal favorites in each subject area. The prices I've listed are based on averages taken from the catalogs of companies that sell to educational institutions. (Look in Chapter 20 for a list of my favorite catalogs.)

General Reference

My First Incredible Amazing Dictionary (Dorling Kindersley, $30, early elementary)

I love the crisp visual elements of this dictionary. Dorling Kindersley seems to have mastered the concept of clear, concise examples. This dictionary also has three games that focus on letter sounds, spelling, and beginning reading skills. I'd say that this is the perfect first dictionary for the elementary classroom

First Connections: The Golden Book Encyclopedia (Hartley, $110, elementary)

A totally interactive learning experience (with more than 1,500 articles and 2,700 graphics) makes this first encyclopedia a top seller. My favorite aspect is the constantly available notebook that enables students to jot down information and either copy it into another application or print it at a later time. A bookmark function also allows students to mark one article before going on to another one. This makes returning to previously viewed entries easy.

Grolier Multimedia Encyclopedia (Grolier, $85, upper elementary-high school)

This encyclopedia is a little easier to use than most of the other CD encyclopedia offerings and is considered by many teachers to be the most educational of the CD encyclopedias currently available. The articles are super! I'm amazed at the depth of the information and the number of multimedia links found within this CD. The abundant QuickTime movies and photos are perfect for multimedia presentations.

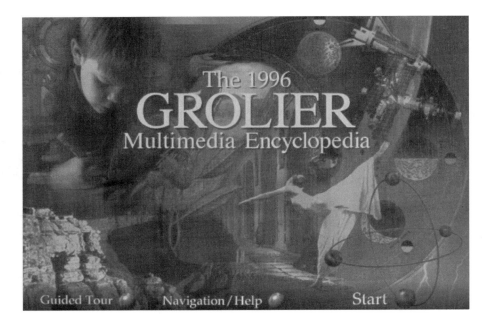

Encarta '95 (Microsoft, $70, upper elementary-high school)

This encyclopedia is visually appealing and easy to use. The interface is a little difficult to manipulate at first; but after the interface is mastered, the wealth of multimedia components found in *Encarta '95* is a great reward for the effort. Access to the photo or QuickTime movie you're looking for is easy. I love the timeline feature, which in itself is a great teaching tool.

3-D Atlas (EA* Kids, $75, upper elementary-high school)

3-D Atlas takes the standard paper-based atlas to the mat. You have the power to rotate a three-dimensional version of the globe, zoom in on areas you wish to explore, and access political, geographical, and environmental data. Add satellite images and QuickTime movies that take you to the action, and you get an idea of how incredible this CD really is.

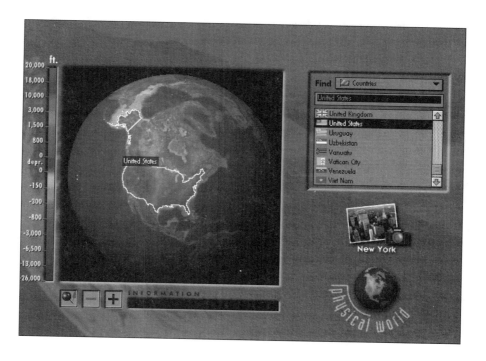

Time Almanac, Reference Edition (Brøderbund, $59, elementary-high school)

This CD came as part of a reference bundle with one of my school's new computers. I was pleasantly surprised by the amount of information this one CD held. *Time Almanac* features information from weekly issues of *Time* for the years 1989 through 1994 and then condenses information decade-by-decade for the years 1920 through 1989. The Top Stories section of each decade's screen quickly shows the students what QuickTime movies or photos are available for that time period.

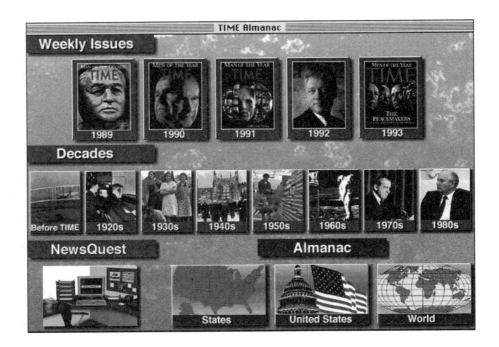

Our Times: The Multimedia Encyclopedia of the 20th Century (Vicarious, $70, middle-high school)

James Earl Jones narrates this new reference source. The CD is very easy to maneuver and features over 52,000 articles. This CD is a combination of the book *Our Times* and the *Columbia Encyclopedia* (5th edition). I had a good time "playing" with this CD and also learned quite a bit along the way! Look for a demo version on the *Mac Multimedia For Teachers CD*.

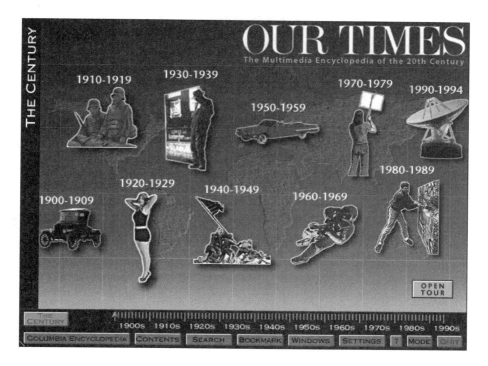

Language Arts

Imagination Express (EdMark, $40, elementary-middle school)

Kids find this one fun, fun, fun! With a little effort and a lot of creativity, children can create their own e-books complete with animated characters and cool sound effects — look out Brøderbund! Currently you may purchase three scenarios (sold separately): Castle, Neighborhood, and Rainforest. Each scenario comes with a wide selection of background scenes and stamps to illustrate your story.

KidWorks 2 (Davidson, $42, elementary)

This title is one of those "must haves" that every school seems to end up buying eventually. Yes, it does have art components similar to those components that are found in *KidPix;* however, the true strength of this program lies within its writing component. There are a number of reasons I love to let youngsters work with this program: the large font that resembles perfect manuscript print, the icons for words from each part of speech (a picture of the sun can be found in the noun box), the verbal capability of these icons, and (above all) the fact that this program will read children's stories back to them!

Reader Rabbit's Interactive Reading Journey (The Learning Company, $85, elementary)

Reader Rabbit is one bunny who's been around the education block a time or two. This new and improved Reader Rabbit, though, has taken a few steroids and has become a very interactive little fellow. The reading journey takes viewers through a magical land as Reader Rabbit introduces them to reading through a series of phonetic activities and mini-reading books. I especially like the fact that this program can be set up to require mastery at one level before readers can move on to the next level. The CD comes packaged with 40 printed storybooks.

Brøderbund's Living Book Series (Brøderbund, $40 per title, elementary)

I've already mentioned these e-books in a couple of other places within this supreme work (see Chapters 17 and 18 for details). Just know that these titles are too incredible to explain with the written word and take a look at the demonstration samples provided on the *Mac Multimedia For Teachers CD*.

Kid Phonics (Davidson, $65, early elementary)

This program is great for kindergarten and first-grade teachers who believe in a strong phonics background for early readers. The activities are so much fun that your students will forget that they are learning. The listening-comprehension skills that students will acquire is an added bonus. The Word Builder and Sentence Builder activities are better than any silly ol' worksheet.

Math

Countdown (Voyager, $30, early elementary)

I just love the graphics on this CD, and the QuickTime movies make the counting process very realistic. The hands-on manipulation aspect of this CD is sure to appeal to educators. I also like the fact that the objects used are things kids see around them every day. After younger children have used this game to master number concepts and counting, you can easily adjust the difficulty level or work on other skills such as patterns and estimation strategies.

Counting on Frank (Creative Wonders, $40, elementary)

Word problems and estimation strategies are the strong points of this title. Online help is available whenever you need a little strategy assistance to help solve a problem. The funny problems encountered are based around scenarios that help students realize the importance of math in their everyday lives.

The Cruncher (Davidson, $35, upper elementary-middle school)

Davidson has managed to take something as boring as a spreadsheet and turn it into a fun and interactive learning experience. This program even includes a talking tutorial to talk students through the basics. The project templates (Party Planner, Surveys, Baseball Statistics, and much more) that are included will give your students a good place to start, and *their* enthusiasm will keep *you* going!

How Many Bugs in a Box? (Simon and Schuster Interactive, $45, early elementary)

Based around David A. Carter's best-selling pop-up book, this interactive CD is a great vehicle for teaching early number concepts. My daughter loves the attribute activities, the sorting games, and the number mazes. This CD teaches difficult early math concepts in a way that even the youngest user can comprehend.

Math Workshop (Brøderbund, $45, elementary)

You get a lot of bang for your buck with this cool title. Seven rooms are in this math-lab-of-sorts, and each room is filled with activities that make learning the basics a little less painful. I love the spatial orientation, estimation, and problem-solving aspects of this program — all of which are rare in most math software. The teachers I've talked with like the fact that this program has a wide variety of difficulty levels, and it can keep track of up to 40 students' scores.

Science

A.D.A.M. The Inside Story (Brøderbund, $40, upper elementary-high school)

Remember those acetate overlays in the middle of your high school biology textbook? Well, if you can imagine what your book would have been like if those overlays had been computerized and had been given a sense of humor, you'll have an insight into the appeal of *A.D.A.M.* After you've used this CD, you'll have no doubt as to why it has remained at the top of all the recommended software lists.

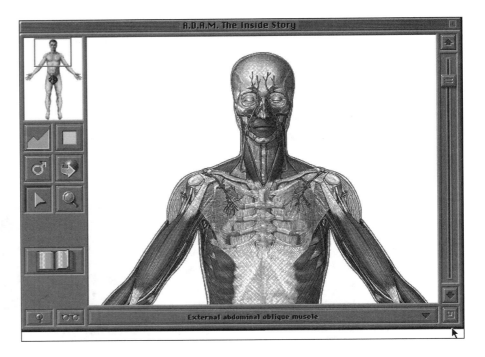

Oceans Below (The Software ToolWorks, $30, elementary-high school)

If you're a diver, if you have ever wanted to go diving, or if you simply teach an ocean unit every year, this CD is for you. The action whisks you away to some of the most popular diving spots around the world — all free of charge and without a travel agent to bother you! During your dive, you are free to explore and learn about the ocean life that surrounds you. The narrated video segments are very informative.

Space Shuttle (MindScape, $30, elementary-middle school)

How would you like your students to be able to take part in an actual NASA shuttle flight? (I know: Don't tempt you. There are days when I, too, would have sent my entire class straight to the moon.) Anyway, this CD is *so* realistic. Students can view launch preparations, practice going on space walks, experience a launch, and much more with the assistance of more than 45 minutes of video footage. All these adventures combine to make for a very realistic learning experience.

The Animals! (Mindscape, $28, elementary-middle school)

We have this CD available for use on six computers in our media center. Teachers are constantly bringing in small groups of children to enjoy a tour of the San Diego Zoo. What I like best about this CD is the capability to easily access information about a specific animal or the animal life in a specific area of the world. It takes only seconds to find out if there's a video, snapshot, or some written text available about a topic. To just sit and explore your way through the entire zoo is also great fun.

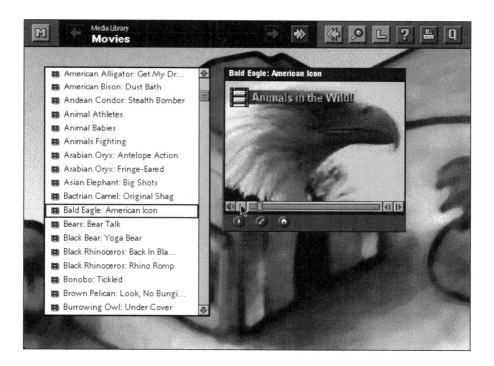

How Your Body Works (Mindscape, $40, elementary-middle school)

This CD is new on the market, and it amazes everyone who sees it. The CD's user-friendly aspect is apparent from the start, and the CD's appeal just grows from there. I love the video segments that are part of the Body Tours; and the Disorders file was eye-opening as well. I think that this CD will be giving the ever-popular *A.D.A.M.* series a run for it's money in the years to come.

3-D Dinosaur (Knowledge Adventure, $48, elementary-middle school)

You won't be able to pull kids away from this CD. The full-motion video is amazing. Some 3-D glasses come with the CD; and the 3-D Museum Tour, which you control with a mouse, makes this dino CD rise above the rest. There's also a "Dino-pedia" for those of you who lean towards the more standard forms of research.

RedShift (Maris, $55, middle-high school)

This simulation CD takes viewers on a space voyage. The graphics (more than 700 photos) are incredible, and the astronomy information is top-notch. On the research side, hypertext links feature more than 2,000 entries. This CD also features detailed surface maps of the earth, the earth's moon, and Mars. Viewers can even capture their travels as a QuickTime movie.

What Is a Bellybutton? (Time/Life IVI Publishing, $35, early elementary)

Too cute! If you're tired of answering all those *why* questions (that sometimes even *you* don't know the answer to), pop in this CD and give your weary old brain a rest! My daughter was totally enthralled by this cartoon-like CD that takes a child through a day full of questions and delivers answers that are very easy to understand. The entertaining manner of this CD makes the information *stick*.

Social Studies/History

Vital Links — A Multimedia History of the U.S. (Davidson, $465, middle-high school)

Vital Links was created by Davidson and Addison-Wesley as a way to mainstream multimedia technology into the everyday curriculum. This intensive and comprehensive program has well over a year's worth of history lessons that bring US history alive from precolonization through the present.

Multimedia projects (this program is a program after my own heart) are at the center of this great package. There are productivity tools that allow students to create spreadsheets, word processing documents, artwork, and presentations that enhance the in-depth learning that takes place throughout the program.

I know that you're probably wondering, "Why is this program so expensive?" Well, for that one low price, you get the following: 1 laser disc, 1 videotape, a set of 5 CD-ROMs, 30 *Vital Links Chronicles* newspapers, a teacher's guide, a user's guide, and training guides.

Where in the World is Carmen Sandiego? (Brøderbund, $50, upper elementary-middle school)

Turn on any public television station and you're bound to hear the catchy little jingle that drives parents crazy but gets children excited about map-and-social-studies skills. Carmen is an evil villain who travels all around the world and does terrible things. By answering questions with the help of clues based on geographic, historical, and map-skills information, students are put to the ultimate challenge of tracking down Carmen and her gang.

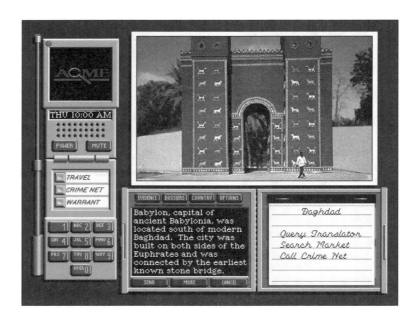

JFK Assassination: A Visual Investigation (Medio Multimedia, $60, middle-high school)

Students become active participants in the investigation of the murder of President John F. Kennedy. This CD contains information used by the Warren Commission as well as the infamous video footage of the shooting. Students use all the information to come up with their own conclusions.

The Oregon Trail II (MECC, $35, upper elementary-middle school)

If you haven't seen this latest version of one of the oldest Apple programs still around, you need to get a copy of it. The original version remained a top seller for years, and this new version has already hit the top ten. The premise is a trip to Oregon in the 1800s. Viewers must get their wagon and its passengers there safely. The hunting sequences were my students' favorites. The information is perfect for studying about the period of westward expansion.

Secrets of the Pyramids (Mindscape, $32, elementary-middle school)

I had to relearn all about ancient Egypt in order to teach the subject to my third grade class a few years ago after the higher-ups decided that ancient civilizations needed to be a part of an eight-year-old's curriculum. I wish I'd had this CD then. By using this CD, students can take a journey inside a pyramid, view animated video of how the pyramids were built, examine Egyptian burial rituals, and much more.

Who Built America? (Voyager, $50, middle school-high school)

There's something about historical video clips that just blows me away. Maybe I am so enthusiastic about such video clips because I didn't have access to them when I was younger; I could only hear about historical happenings or read about them in books. This CD explores the rich texture of America at the turn of the century by using great video, informative audio, and authentic photos from that time period. The information is given from the viewpoint of ordinary Americans, both native-born and immigrant, who had a hand in shaping America as we know it today.

CNN Time Capsule 1994 (Brøderbund, $29, middle school)

This CD is a multimedia yearbook of sorts, and it features 100 of what CNN determined were the year's most newsworthy events. Each of the events (ranging from the death of Jacqueline Kennedy Onassis to the Nancy Kerrigan fiasco) has been turned into its own little feature story on this CD. The film footage is wonderful — but, then again, that's what we expect from CNN. For the price, I'd like to get one of these yearbooks each year for myself. Then when I'm one of those old, gray-haired, retired schoolteachers, I can pop it in and reflect on the world as it was.

Critical Thinking/Problem Solving

Super Solvers Gizmos & Gadgets! (The Learning Company, $45, elementary-middle school)

This program might be considered a junior version of *Widget Workshop.* The environment in this CD is more controlled, and the activities are less open-ended. Still, the basic concepts are the same: experimentation and manipulation. The arcade-like games will satisfy younger minds, but the puzzles will pose more of a challenge.

The Lost Mind of Dr. Brain (Sierra Online, $50, middle school-high school)

This game is so challenging that even my husband (a noncomputer type) loves it! The ability-level-setting feature makes it a great CD for a wide range of ages. In order to restore Dr. Brain's mind, one must solve ten different puzzles. This CD may send steam from your students' ears, but it will keep them on their toes; and maybe, just maybe, some of that intense thought will carry over to more traditional classroom subjects.

Widget Workshop (Maxis, $45, upper elementary-middle school)

Imagine inheriting a garage full of junk from a scientist and then being left alone in that garage for a few days, and you'll have an idea of the concepts behind *Widget Workshop:* free exploration and manipulation of a large variety of parts and pieces. Students explore a myriad of scientific principles while the CD fosters their senses of adventure and curiosity. What happens if you hook a rubber band around a gear that's connected to a battery that's connected to a fuse that's connected to a . . .? Get *Widget Workshop* and find out!

SimCity 2000 (Maxis, $70, middle school-high school) and *SimTown* (Maxis, $40, elementary school)

SimCity 2000 challenges students by requiring them to take raw land and develop a prosperous city on it. *SimTown* is the junior version of this game. Both games are designed to teach basic economics, ecology, and long-term planning in a hands-on environment. *SimCity 2000* also has the added realism of natural disasters.

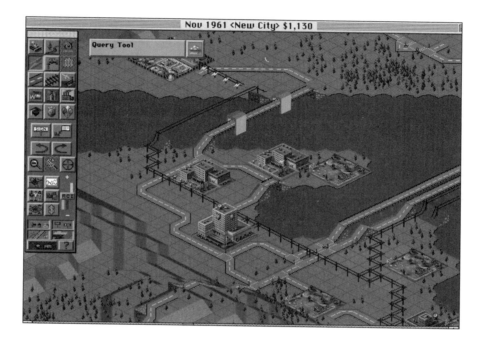

Other Lists Found within This Book

- ✔ Check Chapter 17 for great multimedia titles and cool peripherals for preschoolers.

- ✔ Chapter 18 has some great ideas for using multimedia with special education students.

- ✔ Chapter 7 has a list of my favorite laser disc titles.

- ✔ Software programs to help you develop multimedia presentations are highlighted in Chapters 8 through 10.

- ✔ Super clip art, photo images, fonts, graphics, and movie sources are listed in Chapter 16.

- ✔ Little Picassos will like the drawing and painting programs noted in Chapter 5.

Chapter 16

Top Ten Resources for Multimedia Sound, Video, and Graphics

● ●

1'm a firm believer in asking children to create their own artwork, movies, and sound effects for their multimedia productions. After all, they are children; we shouldn't expect their production to be on the same level as a New York City design firm. However, there are times when asking children to create their own work might be expecting too much of them — such as those times when they need a map of the area Hitler had conquered before the end of World War II or when they'd like to include portions of a speech that Richard Nixon gave before resigning the presidency. In cases like these, I guess I'd give in and let the little darlings use an outside resource. Here's a list of my ten favorite resources. (See Chapter 20 for a list of mail-order companies that carry the products in this chapter.)

MacWarehouse's Ultimate Desktop Publishing Bundle

MacWarehouse, $50

MacWarehouse created this bundle from some of its best-selling clip CDs. Here's what you get for this one low price: *Corel Gallery* (10,000 clip art images), *Corel Professional Photo Sampler* (100 Kodak photo CD images), *SoftKey's Photo Library* (2,500 photos), *Media Clip's World View* (really cool images and QuickTime movies), *Key Fonts Professional* (1,555 typefaces), *SoftKey's ClipArt Library* (3,000 hand-drawn color clip art masterpieces), and *Key ClipMaster Professional* (5,000 pieces of clip art). And all these materials are royalty-free!

K–12 Graphics Collection (Volumes 1 and 2)

Creative Pursuits, $33

These collections are jam-packed with clip art that meets the needs of just about every area of education. The Mac version comes with all the files already in PICT format so that they're ready to use with the following programs: *The Writing Center, ClarisWorks, KidWorks 2, KidPix, HyperStudio,* and more. Volume I has art covering such categories as animals, dinosaurs, history, human anatomy, insects, landmarks, literature, and more. Volume II's art covers awards, celebrations, classroom, holidays, kids, make-believe, and more.

ClipSounds

Monarch, $45

These sounds come in two different packages: one version works with *The Writing Center,* and a second (multimedia) version works with *HyperStudio* and *Multimedia Workshop.* There are more than 80 copy-and-paste sounds in categories such as nature, animals, transportation, sports, history, fantasy, and more.

America Online

If you have America Online, there are tons of sounds, QuickTime movies, photos, and graphics that are easy to download. The easiest place to find this wealth of resources is within the Computing forum (keyword **Computing**). Then there are other places, such as the ABC forum (keyword **ABC**), where you can get pictures of your favorite stars or still shots from the latest movies. Cruise around and take a peek — you'll be pleasantly surprised by what you find.

Corel Stock Photo Library

Corel, $699

I know the price seems high, but you get 200 CDs for that price — with a total of 20,000 photo images! The images are all royalty-free, so you don't have to worry about copyright infringement, and they're saved in Kodak photo CD format. To make accessing the photo you want a little easier, the library comes with an index CD and a full-color reference manual.

ClickART Instant Images

T/Maker, $30 – $60

T/Maker has put together a variety of clip art packages with different themes to meet your needs. The *Cartoon Fun 5 Pak* has over 500 cartoons from five of the funniest cartoonists and comes with 10 bonus fonts as well. Your front-office folks will love the *Newsletter Art* package, which also comes with a few cartoons to liven up even the most boring announcements. I like the *Art Parts* package the best. The clip art looks as if you took the time to draw the images yourself — very stylish!

Kaboom!

Nova Development, $40

You can have over 150 unique sounds that can be used to customize your Mac's functions (you may decide to attach the sound of a cow mooing when you empty the trash) or to use within your multimedia presentations. *Kaboom!* also comes with a sound editing program that lets you edit your *Kaboom!* sounds or edit sounds that you've recorded on your own.

Best of K–12 Graphics CD

Software Sense, $46

This CD has been a top seller at Educational Resources for a long time. It contains more than 1,000 color and black-and-white graphics. Teachers love this collection because of the wide variety of graphics it features.

School Font Collection

Mountain Lake Software, $37

Someone should have come up with this collection a long time ago — and then installed it on every Mac that comes into a school! The fonts in this collection mirror those we spend hours teaching the children to create with a #2 pencil. There are traditional manuscript and cursive fonts as well as D'Nealian-style letters. The letters are crisp and easy to read — important aspects in multimedia.

Check the Software That You're Using

Each time software manufacturers upgrade their products, they add more goodies. *HyperStudio* recently released Version 3.0, which is filled with cool sounds and graphics. *ClarisWorks,* in its latest version, also contains a great deal of clip art. What I'm trying to tell you is this: Check out what you've already got in the closet before you go shopping for new clothes. In Appendix B, I've included a visual reference of all the graphics included in *HyperStudio* and *KidPix Studio* — so take a look.

The 5th Wave By Rich Tennant

"Remember, Charles and Di can be pasted next to anyone but each other, and your Elvis should appear bald and slightly hunched- nice Big Foot, Brad- keep your two-headed animals in the shadows and your alien spacecrafts crisp and defined."

Chapter 17
Top Ten (or More) Reasons Preschoolers Love Multimedia

1'll never forget the evening that my daughter Jessie came running into the kitchen and said, in an exasperated tone, "Mommy, I can't get out of this program!" This may not seem like such an unordinary exclamation; however, the fact that she was barely three years old at the time makes it quite *extra* ordinary.

Life is so different for today's children. Jessie's daycare center classroom has six computers, and computer education is a part of the center's curriculum for both the three- and the four-year-olds' classrooms!

Full-day kindergarten programs are now commonplace in most of today's elementary schools; and many school systems, such as the one I work for, are starting early-learning programs for all four-year-olds. The research isn't in yet on what effect all this early classroom learning and technology will have on our children. All I can tell you from experience is that my two preschoolers love the computer and seem to pick up quickly on the educational elements offered — as long as I keep them supplied with plenty of high-quality software programs and CD-ROM titles.

The software companies have quickly realized the growth in the number of preschoolers who have access to computers. The market is flooded with early-learning CD-ROMs, software, and devices designed that make it easier for little hands to use the computer. In this chapter, I've listed what I feel are the highlights (yes, there are more than ten) of the multimedia computing scene for the younger set.

kidBoard

kidBoard, $100

This standard QWERTY keyboard was created with the help of preschool teachers. It's color coded for left hand and right hand. The keys also have pictures (icons) of items that match the letter on the key (the *A* key has an apple, the *S* key has a star, and so forth). These icons are great reminders for kids who are in the early stages of reading.

kidBoard (photo courtesy of kidBoard, Inc.)

Trackballs

For children as well as for adults, learning how to use a mouse is often one of the most difficult aspects of learning how to use the computer. Many parents choose a trackball (rather than a mouse) as the input device of choice for their preschool children. A trackball is something like an inverted mouse. The base is stationary, and the cursor is moved by rolling the ball located on the top of the base.

kidDraw

kidDraw, $130

This digitizing tablet was designed especially for children ages two and older. The tablet is durable, has an attached red stylus, and works with most of the popular computer-drawing programs. In addition, the tablet comes with a coloring/tracing book containing 100 illustrations for kids to trace, color, or customize. It also has a cool little hook on the back that props the tablet up like an easel, angling it in a way that creates a more comfortable work environment for the younger set.

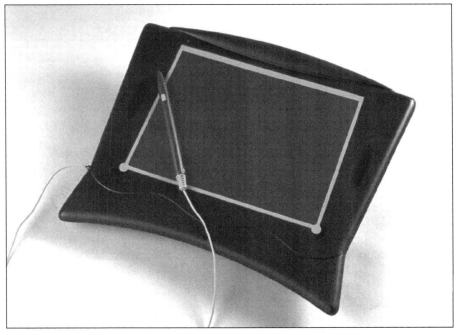

kidDraw (photo courtesy of kidBoard, Inc.)

Edmark's TouchWindow

Edmark, $300

This window attaches to the front of a computer screen and allows the viewer to simply touch the window in order to access commands. The TouchWindow package comes with the software necessary to run the window, and the program even includes a screen that allows the user to customize the pressure setting so that even the lightest touch will be accepted.

Brøderbund's Living Books

Brøderbund, $35 per title (CD)

I own every title in this series! Brøderbund has made deals with some of the more popular children's authors and has turned their stories into creative electronic masterpieces. These e-books (electronic books) are so good that adults often find themselves "playing" within their pages. Each of the books also includes a Spanish-language version on the same CD. Current titles in the series include:

- *Arthur's Birthday* by Marc Brown
- *Arthur's Teacher Trouble* by Marc Brown
- *The Berenstain Bears Get in a Fight* by Stan and Jan Berenstain
- *Dr. Seuss's ABC* by Dr. Seuss
- *Harry and the Haunted House* by Mark Schlichting
- *Just Grandma and Me* by Mercer Mayer
- *Little Monster at School* by Mercer Mayer
- *The New Kid on the Block* by Jack Prelutsky
- *Ruff's Bone* by Eli Noyes
- *The Tortoise and the Hare* (one of Aesop's fables)

KidPix Studio

Brøderbund, $45 (CD)

This program serves as a great early introduction to multimedia production. Creativity rules as children experiment with the huge selection of drawing, painting, animation, and movie tools that this program provides. Kids love the sound effects of each of the tools. And the ability to turn their creations into slide shows to share with others is another plus. My favorite component has to be the *Moopies,* where kids can create pictures and add animation with very little effort.

With animation, you can make the rain look like it's falling.

Kid Phonics

Davidson, $75 (CD)

I previewed this brand-new CD while writing this book. I was completely blown away by the solid phonics base this program provides. I've long been a believer that phonics holds a very important place in the teaching of basic reading skills, and *Kid Phonics* provides a very good jumping-off point for preschoolers embarking on the adventure of reading. The games stress the differences between letter sounds and require the user to listen carefully (a skill all mothers of preschoolers likes to see stressed) in order to ascertain the correct answer. I particularly liked the Word Builder activity where different endings or beginnings of words can be manipulated.

JumpStart Kindergarten

Knowledge Adventure, $45 (CD)

I was so excited to learn that a Mac version of this critically acclaimed program would soon be on the market. There are also plans for *JumpStart PreSchool* and *JumpStart First Grade.* This CD features 13 fun and exciting early-learning activities that are sure to keep any preschooler entertained. The educational elements highlighted include telling time, math, reading, and language arts.

Millie's Math House, Bailey's Book House, and Sammy's Science House

Edmark, $35 each (disk)

These three titles should be mandatory requirements in any preschool education program. I love the stuff the Edmark people produce because I can tell that they have educators guiding the work. Each of these programs has a variety of challenging games and difficulty levels that will help preschoolers learn basic skills in a fun atmosphere.

Thinkin' Things Collection 1

Edmark, $40 (disk)

Thinkin' Things is another great package from Edmark that's well worth the cost. Each of the activities in the program highlights problem-solving and critical-thinking skills — you know, the areas that your administrators highlight as needing the most improvement on those standardized test score sheets. Anyway, the games on this CD are so much fun that you'll find yourself spending time on the computer after school — the background music for the spatial awareness game is very New Age.

The Playroom

Brøderbund, $30 (disk)

Counting, early math skills, telling time, letter recognition, beginning spelling, and early reading skills are all presented within this program, and each game is accessible from a cool little playroom! Nearly all of the games have adjustable skill levels, and maneuvering between games is easy for most children. This program was one of the first high-quality early-learning packages, and it should remain on the list of bestsellers for some time to come.

Disney's Aladdin Activity Center and The Lion King

Disney, $30 each (CD)

Disney has entered the CD market with the style and appeal you'd expect. This new line of CD-ROM titles is the only series that has come close to matching the success of Brøderbund's Living Books. The animation is flawless, as are the sound effects. The *Aladdin Activity Center* CD has great early-learning games and puzzles, and *The Lion King* is presented as a story. The best feature on *The Lion King* is Rafiki, the wise old baboon. After a page has been read by the narrator, young children can highlight a word they might not know the meaning of and then click Rafiki; he will say the word again and use it in a sentence to help them understand its meaning and usage. This "word understanding" feature is not found in the Brøderbund books.

Simba and his best friend Nala told Zazu they were going to the watering hole. They were really planning to go to the elephant graveyard! Along the way the cubs teased Zazu.

My First Incredible Amazing Dictionary

Houghton Mifflin, $30 (CD)

I needed this dictionary when I was a child. I loved words and was constantly asking what different words meant — then I'd walk around using the words (sometimes in the correct context) for days. (I guess my mother would have really liked for me to have had access to this CD!) There are 1,000 words in this electronic dictionary for kids, and the dictionary is full of illustrations, animation, and narration. A couple of fun games that reinforce dictionary skills and early reading skills are also included on this CD.

How Many Bugs in a Box?

Simon & Schuster Interactive, $40 (CD)

This CD is based on David Carter's books about insects. The CD has eight different games highlighting concepts such as counting, observation, sequencing, memory, attributes, charting, matching, and sorting. My personal favorite is Bugs on a Table. In this game, kids are introduced to charts and participate in some fun sorting challenges.

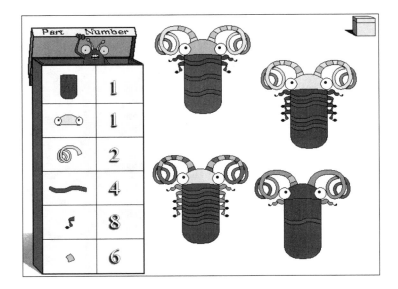

Incredible inserts

As I've mentioned in numerous areas of this book, many of the software companies are starting to employ educators (yeah, I'm talking teachers). Brøderbund has put its teachers to work, and the results can now be seen in the form of educational extension booklets inserted with each *Living Books* purchase. These pamphlet-style inserts contain great educational activities that take the learning beyond the CD and into the home or classroom.

Countdown

Voyager, $30 (CD)

I just love the graphics on this CD, and the QuickTime movies make the counting process very realistic. The hands-on manipulation aspect of this CD is sure to appeal to educators. I also like the fact that the objects used are things kids see around them every day. After younger children have used this game to master number concepts and counting, you can easily adjust the difficulty level of the game or use it to work on other skills such as patterns and estimation strategies.

Chapter 18

Top Ten Reasons Multimedia Is Great for Special Education

• •

1 believe that special education teachers have already earned their spots in heaven. The patience and understanding that these individuals exhibit on a daily basis simply amazes a mere mortal like me. I admire these teachers, and I'm happy to say that this chapter mentions a few products that might make their jobs a little easier.

The Alliance for Technology Access

This organization provides information on technology access for the mentally and physically impaired. These dedicated folks can provide you with a wealth of great stuff — like how to find special education funding! The Alliance for Technology Access also has over 45 satellite centers across the country that are staffed with well-informed people who are ready to help you meet the needs of your special education students. They also spend a great deal of time conducting workshops and inservices across the country.

Call or write and find out if there's a center close to you or order the great book, *Computer Resources for People With Disabilities*. You can contact The Alliance for Technology Access at 2173 East Francisco, Suite 11, San Rafael, CA 94901 (415-455-4575).

Dunamis

Dunamis is a company located in my hometown, Atlanta. This small company was started by Al Rudnik and Ben Satterfield; both are fathers of special needs children. The tireless efforts of these two men have produced two popular technological adaptations for disabled learners, the PowerPad and *StackShop*.

The PowerPad is a laptop touch tablet that works along with *HyperStudio* stacks that are created with *StackShop* software. By using *StackShop* software with *HyperStudio*, you can create customized stacks on any area of study. *StackShop* enables you to program different areas of the computer screen to respond to a simple touch on the PowerPad. This setup is great for those students who have disabilities that prevent them from using a keyboard, a mouse, or a trackball.

You can contact Dunamis for more information at 800-828-2443.

Poor Richard's Publishing

Richard Wanderman started this company three years ago as a way of distributing regular and special education *HyperCard* stacks. (*HyperCard* is a program that is very similar to *HyperStudio*.) Richard, himself, is dyslexic and shares the pain of those students who struggle through school. After he reached the college level, his use of technology helped him compensate for a multitude of problems. In addition to operating Poor Richard's Publishing, Richard also stays busy as an internationally recognized expert consultant in the area of educational technology.

I've included Richard's catalog and a few sample stacks on the bonus CD. As you'll see, all of his stacks are reasonably priced at a mere $20 each. I think that special education teachers will be especially interested in the stack titled "Growing Up with a Learning Disability."

If you'd like to contact Richard yourself, you can reach him on America Online. His screen name is **rwanderman**.

Edmark's TouchWindow

TouchWindow $300

This invention has already been mentioned in a number of other areas within this book. The TouchWindow is a screen of sorts that fits over the front of your computer's monitor. The software provided with the window equips your computer with the information needed to respond to touches on the screen for input (in place of a more traditional device such as a mouse or a trackball). Instead of clicking, students can point to the item that they wish to select. The TouchWindow has been used extensively, and with great success, in the special education program at my school.

Trackballs

Using a mouse is probably one of the most frustrating skills to master when learning basic computer skills. Imagine how difficult this task might be to a special education student. A trackball can be the answer for many special education students. The trackball's stationary base holds a rotating ball (like a mouse turned upside down). The movements of the ball control the cursor movements on the screen. Most trackballs come with software that enables you to increase the size of the cursor on the screen as well as control the rate of movement of the rotating ball itself.

Specialized Keyboards

IntelliTools has been creating adaptive computer equipment since 1979. Their two most popular products are IntelliKeys and *IntelliPics*. IntelliKeys, an extremely flexible keyboard, comes with overlays that can give the keyboard a different "face." One student might use IntelliKeys with oversized letters arranged in alphabetical order, while another student might interact with pictures of animals on an overlay. IntelliKeys can even be used as a training device for students who cannot speak!

IntelliPics is a multimedia authoring program designed for special education teachers. This program is great for creating lessons tailored specifically to the needs of a child with a disability. You can then use the activities with IntelliKeys, a mouse, the TouchWindow, or the regular keyboard.

For more information or the name of a local dealer, call 800-899-6687.

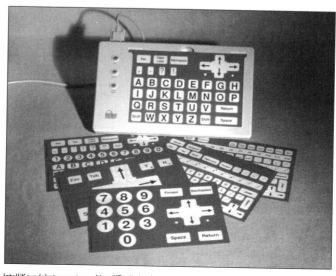

IntelliKeys (photo courtesy of IntelliTools, Inc.)

Hats off to Edmark and Brøderbund

Edmark and Brøderbund were the first mainstream software companies to understand the needs of special education students. These wonderful companies recently modified many of their software programs (including the ever-popular *Where in the World is Carmen Sandiego?*) so that they can be adjusted to different developmental levels. Look for other companies to follow suit soon.

Don Johnston Incorporated

Don Johnston had learning disabilities as a child and had to create his own compensation techniques that eventually enabled him to overcome his disability. That memory was the inspiration behind Don Johnston Incorporated.

Ke:nx is Don Johnston's claim to fame and one of the most popular alternative keyboard devices. It has a built-in mouse and speech output features. The big plus here is the fact that the keyboard can operate all standard Mac software, not just software designed for use with the keyboard. That's not to say that this great company hasn't created some great software titles of its own. Among the top sellers are *Co:Writer* (a great word processing program that uses word prediction intelligence for those who struggle with writing) and *K.C. & Clyde in Flyball* (a great little interactive book that focuses on words, context, and multiple-story paths in a manner that learning disabled students can comprehend).

Contact Don Johnston Incorporated at 800-999-4660.

(Photograph reprinted with permission from Don Johnston Incorporated)

CD-ROM Research Material

A few years ago, it would have been considered ludicrous to expect learning-disabled students to conduct in-depth research or prepare in-depth reports. However, having the research material on CDs makes information easy to access. In addition, many CDs have great linking functions that enable students to find related information easily.

As for reports or presentations, easy-to-use software such as *HyperStudio* or *KidPix Studio* makes creating a report fun. Other adaptations mentioned in this chapter can replace frustrating obstacles such as the traditional QWERTY keyboard and the mouse. I see technology as a means to greatly strengthen the knowledge base of most special-needs children.

Headphone Port

The addition of headphone ports may sound like a silly reason for special education teachers to get excited about multimedia technology. However, one of the biggest drawbacks in special education instruction is that you usually have a room full of students with a wide range of needs. That situation means that each student probably has his or her own curriculum that you, the teacher, must develop.

Well, putting a headphone port on the front of all the new Macs was a stroke of genius on Apple's part (older Macs can accommodate a set of headphones via the speaker port on the rear of the computer). Yes, special education teachers would love to use some of the cool multimedia offerings. However, special education students are usually prone to shorter attention spans and higher levels of distractibility. By using a pair of headphones, a teacher can let the computer be used and, at the same time, keep the rest of the classroom on task.

By the way, any old cheap set of headphones (such as the type that are used with the sort of personal radios that people use while jogging) will work — although you may need an adapter. I found some for one dollar per pair and bought enough to equip each of the computers in our Mac lab.

I hope this list has opened a few new doors of opportunity to those of you in special education. There's plenty of room for growth in the areas of special education and technology. Keep your eyes and ears open for new developments on the horizon.

Chapter 19

Top Ten Web Sites for Multimedia and Education

● ●

*H*ere's the part of the book where I admit my weaknesses:

I'm a horrible housekeeper.

I kill houseplants.

I have a dusty treadmill.

I don't know much about the Internet.

But — I'm not ashamed to ask for help.

When I can afford it, I pay someone else to clean my house; I buy silk plants; I try to make it to the gym (when I don't have a writing deadline); and (best of all) I've become a close personal friend of Bard Williams, master of the Internet and author extraordinaire (*The Internet For Teachers,* IDG Books Worldwide, 1995).

Because of my lack of experience on the Internet, Bard graciously agreed to write the balance of this chapter for me. What a friend! I strongly suggest that you purchase *The Internet For Teachers* if you're anything like me and need major amounts of Internet tutoring.

Resources for education and multimedia on the Internet change faster than a speeding school bus. You and your students will find rich repositories of sound, video, picture, and text (which can be useful in crafting multimedia presentations), as well as oodles of samples of student-generated projects. To find a few of the best of these nifty resources, fire up your Web browser (Netscape, Mosaic, and the like), or sign onto an online service such as America Online, and enter the following Web addresses:

Pictures and Sound

There are thousands of sites on the Web. Not only will you find a large selection of traditional educational materials on the Web, but you'll also find some innovative alternatives that aren't available through traditional channels.

Images, Icons, and Flags

This site has a searchable database of clip art organized by subject.

Address: http://www.nosc.mil/planet_earth/images.html

Sandy's Clip Art Server

Here's a great source for clip art and a jumping-off point to other art sources on the Web.

Address: http://www.cs.yale.edu/homes/sjl/clipart.html

The Sound Archives

From barking dogs to classical ditties, you'll find hundreds of public-domain sound samples that are perfect to jazz up any multimedia presentation.

Address: http://www.eecs.nwu.edu/~jmyers/other-sounds.html

Straight to the Source

Jump to these commercial Web sites for great multimedia resources from the originators of multimedia. What a way to get the information you need quickly and straight from the horse's mouth!

Kodak

Here you'll find more digital photos than you can imagine from the makers of the photo CD.

Address: http://www.kodak.com/

Apple Computer, Inc.

Check out Apple's online resources for multimedia and education, including information about building a low-cost multimedia system for your home or school.

Address: http://www.info.apple.com/education/

Silicon Graphics, Inc.

This granddaddy of high-end multimedia presents a dazzling site full of great multimedia resources and examples.

Address: http://www.sgi.com/

Student Samples

These sites contain actual multimedia projects or resources created by students and teachers. This is a great area to cruise just before embarking on a new multimedia project. You and your students will be inspired by the approaches and techniques others have implemented. (Soon you'll be putting your own creations out for the world to view!)

Multimedia Courseware

This City University of New York project was designed to get faculty members interested in alternative methods of content development and delivery. Explore student- and faculty-created multimedia and hypermedia projects at the college level.

Address: http://www.cuny.edu/multimedia/multimedia.html

CTDNet Gallery

This site features student work, including video clips, sound bites, original artwork, and hypermedia.

Address: http://ctdnet.acns.nwu.edu/supp/creative.html

Project Bartleby

This Web site contains hypertext books and poetry. Be sure to check out the Walt Whitman library!

Address: http://www.cc.columbia.edu/acis/bartleby/

ILTWeb K-12 Resources (Columbia University)

Here the Institute for Learning Technologies presents lesson plans and other resources for multimedia in education.

Address: http://www.ilt.columbia.edu/k12/index.html

UCI-Science Education Programs (SEP)

This site features direct links to hundreds of selected K-16 multimedia science gems sorted by subtopic and grade level.

Address: http://www-sci.lib.uci.edu/SEP/SEP.html

Chapter 20

Top Ten Sources for Multimedia Information

Yes, there are other resources out there for you to buy — some of them even have the word *multimedia* in their names. What I'm giving you here are names, telephone numbers, and brief descriptions of the sources that I have found to be beneficial (after weeding through all the other so-called "resources"). Many of the information sources listed here have relevant ties to education. Take a look at the bylines of some of the articles you come across, and you'll see that educators are now calling many of the shots within the publications.

Children's Software Review

(313-480-0040)

Warren Buckleitner started this publication as a means to keep parents informed about available educational software. He uses schools and families as testers to preview the software that he highlights in each issue. I also enjoy reading the Hardware News and Software News sections, where he tells about the latest developments in each area.

Club KidSoft

(800-354-6150)

Some may turn their noses up at my suggesting a mail-order company as a resource. However, this mail-order company is different! Club KidSoft has a team of educators — yes, former teachers and the like — who spend time previewing each software title Club KidSoft features. The team has weeded through the junk, and what the company features in its catalog is usually the cream of the crop. You can also get a preview CD from Club KidSoft for a very reasonable price.

Family PC Magazine

(800-413-9749)

Family PC highlights both Mac and PC products. The real strength of this magazine is found within its activities that are designed to go along with a broad range of software. The editors at *Family PC* have also started to focus more on the use of computers in the classroom — the magazine has even included an article about a middle school in my district! See the coupon in the back of this book for information about subscriptions to this magazine.

Mac Home Journal

(800-800-6542)

This magazine gets better with each issue that I read. For example, I've noticed a great deal of improvement in its educational articles and reviews. *Mac Home Journal* often solicits the opinions of respected educators for articles, and I tend to agree with the opinions of most of the software reviews. See the coupon in the back of this book for information about subscribing to *Mac Home Journal.*

Learning and Leading with Technology

(800-336-5191)

This magazine was formerly titled *Computing Teacher* and is a publication of the ISTE (International Society for Technology in Education), a top-notch group of folks dedicated to our children's education. Each issue combines informative articles by respected educators with software reviews and columns that address the questions posed by teachers interested in the use of technology in education.

HyperStudio Journal

(203-567-1173)

This magazine comes to you in disk form. (The future *is* here!) You simply pop the disk into your computer and install the publication onto your hard drive. The journal is filled with information on making the most of *HyperStudio*. You'll also get some neat backgrounds, clip art, and sound bites with each edition. See the coupon in the back of this book for information about ordering *HyperStudio Journal*.

Educational Resources

(800-624-2926)

This is *the* number one supplier of educational software and computing supplies. Educational Resources also has a "Partnership Plus" program that allows schools to make purchases at lower rates for large orders. Another feature of this company is its kits for staff development.

Learning Services

(West: 800-877-9378; East: 800-877-3278)

Learning Services is also a supplier of software and computer supplies. They aren't as large as Educational Resources, but their prices are very competitive. I always like to call and compare deals before making a purchase for myself or my school. I like the top-sellers lists that Learning Services provides within each category of software (top ten language arts programs, top ten multimedia programs, and so forth).

Electronic Learning Magazine

(800-544-2917)

I first found this magazine in an electronic format on America Online. Its articles address a wide range of educational levels and topics. I also tend to agree with the software and hardware reviews.

AIS Computers

(800-849-4949)

This supplier does an incredible job on software review and demonstration. Its entire staff is dedicated to staying up-to-date on the latest software and CD-ROM titles. (What a job . . . playing on the computer all day!) Anyway, AIS Computers always has someone with firsthand knowledge of the products who can speak to you.

Apple Computer

(800-800-2775)

Yes, this is that *800-Appl* number that everyone tells you to call if you have a question. I used to stay on hold with these people indefinitely. However, they've really gotten things under control recently. The response time is immediate, and their responses are friendly. There's nothing better than getting your information from the source; and in most cases, Apple is the source you need.

Technology & Learning

(800-544-2917)

This magazine features real live classroom teachers in their articles. I love it when someone who is actually spending time in the trenches comes up to give me the *real* lowdown! It's a great source for ideas and inspiration. I think every school needs a subscription to this publication.

Chapter 21

Top Ten Things That Didn't Have a Place in the Other Chapters

• •

*1*t's 2:45 in the afternoon. You've only got 15 minutes until the bell rings, and you still haven't gotten around to that health lesson you put off yesterday. What do you do? Should you put it off for another day in hopes of finding some extra time to devote to the exciting topic of dental hygiene? Or do you give your students a 15-minute lesson (on the proper way to brush their teeth) and pat yourself on the back for making the effort? Hard call, isn't it? But we've all been there before, my friend.

That's what this chapter contains: all of the things that I can't fit in anywhere else in the book but want to make sure that I tell you about before you leave.

Know the Difference Between Freeware and Shareware

If you download software from America Online or some other online service and the software is labeled *freeware,* the software is free — no charge, zip, nada. If the software is labeled *shareware,* the author of the software expects you to pay some type of fee for the software. Most shareware agreements allow you to download and try out the software; and then if you decide to keep it, you simply mail the requested amount (usually under $50) to the shareware's developer. If you decide that you don't like the software, you're asked to dump the entire program in the Trash.

We teachers are usually a pretty law-abiding group of individuals. Don't let me down on this one! If a person takes the time and effort to develop a program and then decides to share it with you, a small fee is the least you can give if you're pleased with the program. A nice note with your payment would also be appreciated.

Honor Copyright Law

Copyright law is very complicated. The main thing you need to know probably sounds like something that you might have said on a number of occasions: If it doesn't belong to you, leave it alone!

Don't scan in images that are copyrighted work, don't include your favorite Barry Manilow tune as background music, and don't use a line from someone else's poem if the poem has been copyrighted.

Along the same lines, copyright your own work. You'd be amazed at the number of folks who will claim your creative thoughts as their own. You probably didn't come by your knowledge easily — take credit for your creations.

Multimedia Is Addictive

After you start on a multimedia project, it will become all-consuming. Thoughts of aspects you want to include, angles you need to cover, and colors that add impact will invade every crevice of your brain. In the middle of the night, you'll wake up trying to recall the name of that *perfect* font you want to use for the opening credits. Don't worry. All these ailments will disappear after you tweak the last frame of your presentation. The symptoms will recur, however, with each new project you attempt; and the symptoms become more severe as your multimedia knowledge level increases.

Buy a Utilities Program

You get a physical examination every year (or you should). When you have a cold, you rest and take fluids. Headaches call for aspirin, and sprained ankles get ice. What I am trying to say is that you take care of your body when it needs your attention. You need to do the same thing for your friend the computer, although you can't tell when your computer is feeling poorly.

Don't wait until the sad Mac icon appears at startup time — you may be too late.

Utilities programs such as *Norton Utilities* or *MacTools* work behind the scenes like 24-hour-doctors-on-call to keep your Mac in tip-top shape. These programs keep tabs on everything that goes on inside your computer's hard plastic shell. If a problem occurs, a screen comes up asking you whether you'd like to fix it.

Frightening fragmentation

Fragmentation occurs during normal computer use. You see, your computer isn't as smart as you'd like it to be. When you save a file, and your hard drive has already used up all its big blocks of open space, your computer breaks the file up (fragments it) into smaller pieces and then saves these pieces in different areas on the hard drive. Now, your Mac does remember where it put the files; however, when it's time to reopen a file, your Mac must perform a quick and frantic act of recovery to put the file back together so that you can open it. Over time, this quick-recovery act becomes more and more difficult. As you fill up space on your hard drive, the computer starts to run out of room to store each of the little pieces of files. And the amount of information the Mac must scan in order to rejoin the files when you open them becomes much larger, as well. In time, a fragmented hard disk will slow down response time and alter your computer's overall performance.

Running a disk defragmentation program is essential. These programs are standard issue with most of the utilities software. A defragmentation program gathers all the scattered bits of files and joins them into one easily accessible clump on your hard drive. Defragmentation makes it quicker and easier for your computer to retrieve and save information.

Don't be surprised if defragmentation takes a long time the first time you defragment your hard drive. (It once took me a full hour!) Defragmentation is really no big deal; the computer does all the work.

Multimedia files are notoriously large and complicated and can quickly slow down a hard drive. Defragmenting once a week will usually suffice for a school computer. Some multimedia gurus recommend defragmenting your hard drive nightly. Defragmenting nightly might not be such a bad idea in the school setting where different groups of children are rotating on and off computers on an hourly basis. The more often you defragment, the quicker the process will be each time.

Two of my favorite functions of these utilities programs are the recover-trashed-items function and the defragmentation function. (See the sidebar "Frightening fragmentation" in this chapter for more information about fragmentation and defragmentation.)

Use Your Video Camera

Don't rely on purchased QuickTime movies to make your presentations complete. Get out that video camera and shoot some of your own movies. The more you use the video camera, the more comfortable you'll become with it. Using a tripod and making good use of the zoom feature will greatly improve your final product. I found a great little book titled *How to Shoot Your Kids on Home Video* by David Hajdu (Newmarket Press, 1988). It's full of useful tips and ideas for creating Hollywood-style effects in your own backyard.

Don't Use Hard Drive Compression Programs

I'm not talking about the same compression programs that I mentioned in Chapter 14 (the compression programs that allow you to stuff individual files). Now I'm talking about compression programs that claim to double your disk capacity. They go by such names as *Stacker* and *Auto Doubler*. These programs work by compressing all your information before the file gets saved and then decompressing the data in order to open up your file again. All this compression and decompression makes for slower reaction times; and in multimedia, time is crucial. You don't want the viewer to wait an extra second to view the cool QuickTime movie you included in your presentation. In other circumstances, such as for simple word processing, these programs might work just fine. Instead of buying compression programs, spend your money for an additional hard drive — you won't regret making *that* purchase.

The Coolest New CD on the Market

If you teach middle school or high school and someone within your school (maybe even you) is responsible for teaching sex education, you've got to give that person a copy of *The Nine Month Miracle* by A.D.A.M. Software. This CD takes you on the journey from conception to birth in a tasteful (and sometimes even humorous) manner. You'll see actual in-body photography, video footage, and medical animation that highlight each stage of a baby's development. I especially like the bonus chapter for younger children, "Emily's New Sister," in which the concepts are brought down a few levels, and the story is told by seven-year-old Emily.

Get Help from Software Manufacturers Online

There isn't a phone in either of the computer labs at my school; and even if there were, I don't think that my colleagues would be too happy if I were to tie up one of only four telephone lines coming into the school while I wait for a technician to answer my software questions. That's why most of the big software companies have created their own online bulletin boards. Getting responses from software manufacturers' online bulletin boards works great! You simply type in your problem (the more specific you are the better), and the technicians write you back with an answer — usually within a 24-hour period. Check out *The Internet For Teachers* (Bard Williams, IDG Books Worldwide) for other helpful sites on the Internet.

Take a Look at the Instruction Manuals and Teachers' Guides

I'm notorious for getting a new piece of software and popping it into my computer without even glancing at the installation directions. However, during the research for this book, I found that many of the larger software companies now employ educators — yes, teachers, hired right out of the classroom — to guide them in the creation of quality software and supplemental materials for educators. Some of the materials, including the directions, actually prove to be very interesting and informative reading. The directions will usually clue you in to some of the keyboard shortcuts that the developers added, and the supplemental materials are often full of neat classroom tie-ins that help validate your increased use of the computer in the everyday functioning of your classroom.

Understand "Public Domain" and "Royalty-Free"

Both of these terms are "good things." A copyrighted work becomes public domain after its copyright expires. The number of years before a copyrighted work comes into the public domain differs based on many variables. However, after a work becomes public domain, anyone can use the work free of charge.

If something is royalty-free, however, the rules are a little different. Royalty-free means that the person or company that provided you with a graphic, a photo, and the like, doesn't expect a royalty or payment each time the work is used. However, some royalty-free items come with disclaimers. This situation makes things really confusing! Some royalty-free work is only royalty-free if you don't profit from its use. The stipulations vary from work to work. In education, it's a pretty good bet that you won't be making money off of your multimedia productions. However, if you created a multimedia school yearbook or sold copies of a multimedia presentation that highlighted your community or state, you might run into some problems. Read all the fine print!

Rebuild Your Desktop

Don't rush out for a hammer and nails. In this case, I'm talking about your computer's desktop. Your desktop file is invisible, yet very important. This iconless file keeps track of what files you have, where they're located, what size they are, the last date they were accessed, and an abundance of other useful information. Here's the kicker: Each time you throw something away, the desktop file still keeps track of it! Over time, your computer's desktop becomes cluttered with information that's no longer relevant (just like your wooden desktop at school becomes cluttered with too many ungraded papers, old pens, and uneaten apples).

Curing this problem is simple. Once a month, when you start up your computer, simply hold down the ⌘ key and Option keys after you see the happy Mac face. Keep holding down these keys until a message appears asking you whether you're sure that you want to rebuild your desktop.

Don't worry about losing the comments in your info windows. Most people never even use these boxes in the first place. Just click OK, and your Mac will do a little housekeeping and recatalog all your files. After all is said and done, the next time you start up your Mac, you should notice things running faster and smoother.

Murphy's Laws for teachers

1. The best students always move away.

2. New students come from schools that don't teach "the basics."

3. Open House inevitably falls on the night Seinfeld is on TV.

4. The problem student in your class will be an administrator's child.

5. The less time you have to make copies, the more the machine will jam.

6. The morning you run out of coffee at home, you'll be observed by your principal.

7. The length of a faculty meeting is usually in direct proportion to the boredom level of the subject.

8. The least appealing room in the school is always the teachers' lounge.

9. The one time you forget to put up your chairs, the custodian will finally decide to come by and vacuum.

10. The more interesting you think that a lesson is, the less your students will pay attention.

Appendix A

A Glossary of Multimedia Terms

accelerator card — This card makes your computer run faster. It usually has a new (faster) processor on it.

access time — This term refers to the amount of time it takes your computer to locate information on a hard drive, CD, or other storage device.

ADB (Apple Desktop Bus) device — Any device that plugs into the same port as your keyboard or mouse. A trackball, digitizer tablet, or TouchWindow would fall into this category.

alert sound — The irritating beep (or other annoying sound) you hear when you do something wrong on the keyboard.

analog — The way audio and video information is processed.

animation — What Disney does better than anyone. Animation occurs when you present a series of graphic images in rapid succession to give the illusion of movement.

attract screen — An initial screen in a multimedia presentation. This screen is designed to *attract* viewers to the presentation. When clicked, the screen usually takes viewers to the start of a presentation.

application — This is what techno-heads call a program.

authoring — Creating something yourself. When you create your own multimedia stacks or presentations using *HyperStudio, KidPix Studio,* or any of the other presentation software titles, you are authoring.

audio bits — This refers to the amount of storage bits that are used by each digital audio sample you take.

audio CD — The LP's worst enemy and ultimate replacement. The disc you put into your stereo if you want to listen to the clearest version of what we affectionately used to call an album.

authentic assessment — A method that involves students in *showing what they know* instead of simply evaluating their knowledge by administering a test. Multimedia authoring is one means of performing authentic assessment.

barcode reader — A device that is used with laser disc players to help access specific segments of the laser disc without having to punch in each barcode number.

Bernoulli — A cartridge-style external storage device (similar to a SyQuest).

binary code — A computer's basic language. It consists of 0s and 1s that are combined into patterns that your computer can read and execute.

bit — The smallest piece of computer information. In binary code, a bit would consist of only one *0* or one *1*.

bitmapped graphic — A method for storing graphics in which each individual pixel's location and color is memorized by the computer.

branching — This term refers to presentations that are nonlinear. If the viewers of a multimedia presentation are allowed to make a choice in the direction of a presentation, then they are branching off the stack of information.

browse — In *HyperStudio*, the browsing tool is the hand icon. You use a browsing tool to actually use or view the stack. When the browsing tool is selected, you can't edit or add to a presentation.

built-in video capture — This means that your computer has a Video In card, and you have the capability to record video images directly into your computer.

button — An area on the screen that is usually represented by an icon or resembles the shape of a button and, when clicked, results in an action of some sort. (A microphone button might produce a sound when clicked, or a right-arrow button might take you to the next screen.)

byte — Eight bits.

caddy — A container of sorts required by some older CD-ROM drives. A CD is placed inside the caddy, and the caddy is then placed in the CD-ROM drive.

CD-ROM — This stands for Compact Disk-Read Only Memory. A CD can be encoded with information only once, but it can be read (or played) over and over again.

CD-ROM burner — This little device will let you create your own CD-ROM.

clip art — Artwork you can purchase and *clip off* for use in desktop publishing or multimedia projects.

Clipboard — This is where the Mac keeps information that you cut or copy. Information stays on the Clipboard until you cut or copy new information or until you turn off your Mac.

clip media — Like clip art, clip media refers simply to media (sound, video, or animation) that you purchase and then clip for use in multimedia projects.

CPU (Central Processing Unit) — The guts of your computer.

digital conversion — The act of converting analog signals (those used by audio and video) into information the computer can understand.

digital cameras — Cameras that convert visual images into digital information that can be imported into a computer.

drawing software — A type of graphics software that produces images similar to those drawn in a freehand style.

drive speed — CD-ROM drives come in a variety of speeds. For example, a double-speed CD-ROM drive spins twice as fast as the single-speed drive in your friendly old automobile's CD player. The faster the CD-ROM drive, the easier it is to access specific information on the CD.

dump to tape/video — Taking what you see on the screen and recording it to video tape. In order to do this, you must have an AV Mac, an AV card, or a presentation system such as the Apple Presentation System.

e-books — Electronic books. The books in the *Brøderbund Living Books* series are probably one of the all-time best examples of e-books.

external hard drive — A hard drive that's connected to your computer externally for use as an alternative means of storage.

external CD-ROM — A CD-ROM drive that is usually purchased separately from — and added to — a computer that didn't come equipped with an internal CD-ROM drive.

flatbed scanner — This scanner looks and acts like that horrible photocopy machine you stand in line to use each day. However, instead of making a copy, a scanner produces a digitized image that you can insert into multimedia presentations or word processing documents.

font — A form of lettering or typeface.

image enhancement software — A type of software that allows you to touch up a photo via a computer. Image enhancement software such as Adobe's *PhotoShop* allows the addition of colors, hand-drawn images, filters, and much more.

input devices — In a classroom, this would more than likely be a #2 pencil. In the world of computers, an input device could be a mouse, a keyboard, a trackball, a digital tablet, or a TouchWindow.

interactive — A program is considered interactive if the user makes decisions about the direction of the program: click here to see a video, click there to go back, and so forth.

internal CD-ROM drive — A CD-ROM drive that was built into the computer.

jewel case — A silly name given to the cheap plastic cases (maybe we should call them *costume* jewel cases) that hold your CDs at the time of purchase.

kilobyte (K) — 1,024 bytes.

kiosk — A freestanding interactive presentation.

Kodak Photo CD — A CD that stores photographic images.

laser disc — What you play in a laser disc player. A laser disc looks something like an old LP, only it holds tons of information and plays back incredibly crisp audio and video information. The information on a laser disc is encoded for easy access to specific areas of information.

laser disc player — This machine looks a lot like your standard VCR. It plays laser discs (see the preceding entry) and can be hooked up to your TV *or* computer.

looping — Playing a multimedia presentation over and over again.

megabyte (MB) — Sometimes referred to in conversation as *megs*. A unit of storage that equals 1,024 kilobytes.

message box — Those annoying little boxes that come up in computer programs and usually ask you to make a decision of some sort, such as *Are you sure you want to quit?*, *The trash can contains.* . . .

MIDI (Musical Instrument Digital Interface) — This acronym refers to a computer code that allows instruments with a MIDI interface to play, record, and store music on a Mac or other MIDI-equipped computer.

narration — Adding voice recordings to enhance a multimedia presentation.

navigation — A term used for working your way through a multimedia presentation.

photo scanner — A scanner that is specially sized to read 3×5 photographs and interpret the images into digital information that a computer can store.

PICT — The most common type of picture file that can be stored on the Mac.

pixel — A single dot that is part of the thousands of dots that make up one image you see on your computer screen.

Power Mac — A really fast Mac; top of the line; capable of leaping tall buildings in a single bound.

PowerBook — What Apple calls its laptop computers.

print to tape — See "dump to tape/video."

QuickTime — A system extension that enables the Mac to combine video, audio, and animation in the same file (known commonly as a QuickTime file).

resolution — The number of pixels-per-inch used to display an image. This number is important (for clarity) when shopping for monitors and scanners.

sampling rate — The rate at which the computer records a sound or video. The higher the sampling rate, the better the result.

scanner — A device that digitizes flat images, such as photos or printed text, so that the images may be saved and used later in other computer applications.

Scrapbook — A cool little part of the Mac's System software that provides a place for you to store all your favorite images, sounds, QuickTime clips, and more for easy access at another time.

slide show — A linear presentation of information that might involve multimedia components. *KidPix2* and *KidPix Studio* are the most popular software programs that can be used to create a slide show. *ClarisWorks* also has a slide show function.

stack — One card (or two or more cards joined together) in a *HyperStudio* or *HyperCard* file.

storyboard — A visual representation of an entire multimedia production, often viewed in comic-strip format or as a series of individual 3×5 cards placed on posterboard. A storyboard is usually created *before* embarking on the computerized version of a presentation. (Check the back of the cheat sheet in the front of the book for a blank storyboard.)

SyQuest — A cartridge-type external storage device.

trackball — An alternative to a mouse as an input device. The screen's cursor is manipulated by rolling a ball that sits in a stationary base.

transition — The elements involved in moving from one slide or card to another during the course of a multimedia presentation. This movement could involve a number of different special effects, such as *fade to black, dissolve,* or *wipe.*

video capture — Recording video to a computer's hard drive.

voice-over — A method for recording voice over existing audio, video, or still images.

Appendix B

Copy, Laminate, and Keep Beside Your Computer

* *

*O*n the next few pages, you'll find a visual reference that will make planning those wonderful multimedia presentations a breeze. I've prodvided you with a copy of each of the graphics found within *HyperStudio* and *KidPix Studio*. I can almost guarantee this appendix to be a classroom timesaver.

Just do as the name says: copy the pages, laminate the pages, and then keep them beside your computer. Then the next time your students are planning a multimedia presentation, have them spend some time going through the pages and planning their graphics before actually getting on the computer. This strategy will help your students become better planners — and will, in turn, cause time spent on the computer to be more productive.

HyperStudio

The latest version of *HyperStudio* (Version 3.0) is chock-full of graphics and fun sounds, all within an easy click of the Media Library. In this appendix, I've included visual images of most of the artwork that you may want to use with your students. The Media Library also contains some additional elements not featured within this appendix — 12 animation clips in the KidAMATION files, 96 great sound clips in the Sound & Music files, and over 145 great backgrounds for your cards in the Screens & Backgrounds files.

Animal kingdom

Arctic Wolf

Atlantic Puffin

Elephant Seal

Emperor Penguin

Polar Bear

Reindeer

Snow Goose

Snowy Owl

Walrus

Golden
Eagle

Arctic Cliffs & Snow

Animal kingdom (continued)

Golden Eagle

Arctic Foreground

Black-chinned
Hummingbird

Arctic Iceflow

Broad-tailed
Hummingbird

Rufous Hummingbird

Nuttalls
Woodpecker

Raven

White-headed
Woodpecker

Williamsons
Sapsucker

Background Clips — Cliffs

Yellow-bellied
Sapsucker

Mountain Peaks

Animal kingdom (continued)

Background Clips — Trees

Faunus
Angelwing

Trees & Bushes

Milberts
Tortoiseshell

Golden Northern
Bumble Bee

Golden
Huntsman
Spider

California Tortoiseshell

Forest Wolf
Spider

California Oak
Gall Wasp

Big Horn Sheep

American Bison

Black Bear

American Elk

Grizzly Bear

American Elk

Grizzly Bear

Yellow-bellied
Marmot

Mule Deer

Hoary
Marmot

Northern Lynx

Animal kingdom (continued)

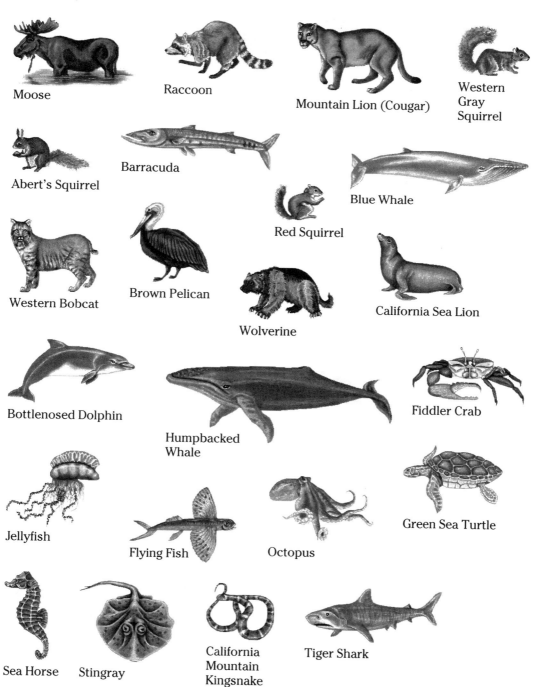

Moose

Raccoon

Mountain Lion (Cougar)

Western Gray Squirrel

Abert's Squirrel

Barracuda

Blue Whale

Red Squirrel

Western Bobcat

Brown Pelican

Wolverine

California Sea Lion

Bottlenosed Dolphin

Humpbacked Whale

Fiddler Crab

Jellyfish

Flying Fish

Octopus

Green Sea Turtle

Sea Horse

Stingray

California Mountain Kingsnake

Tiger Shark

Animal kingdom (continued)

Oregon Ensatina

Arboreal
Salamander

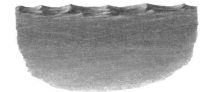

Ocean Surface

Plants & Fish

Sonoran Mountain
Kingsnake

HyperART

Computer 1

Computer 2

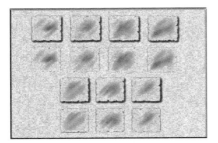

Button Art

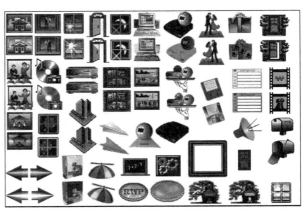

Button Art 2

HyperART (continued)

Addy

Addy With Paws and Cars

Addy — More Paws

More Apps

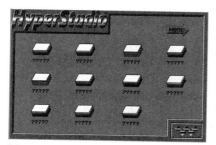

More Stacks

Granite

Dingbats 1

Dingbats 2

HyperART (continued)

Education 1

Icon Library — Clip Art

Education 2

Music

Science

Output

HyperART (continued)

Album

Book

Index

Weekly Pic

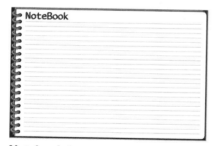

Notebook 1

Notebook 2

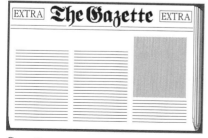

Gazette

World Map

HyperART (continued)

North America

USA

Canada

South America

Antarctica

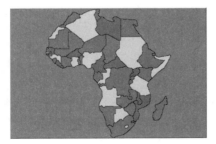

Africa

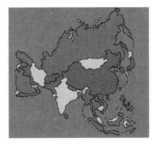

Asia

Australia

Europe

HyperART (continued)

Planets

Solar System

Flags

Tree

Animals

Photo Gallery

The Photo Gallery has a wide variety of photo images that will come in handy with many of your classroom multimedia creations.

Animals

Bear Face

Black Cat

Butterflies

Butterfly on Fern

Camel Family

Cougar Face

Cowboy

Cowboys Herding

Duck

Eagle

Elk

Horse and Baby

Lioness Sleeping

Lions

Llama and Baby

Panda

Parrot

Seagull on Piling

Sheep Grazing

T-Rex Skeleton

Buildings

Barn

Burning House

Ceiling

Church

Football Stadium

Fort Casey Lighthouse

Highrise Construction

House Reflection on Lake

Jefferson Memorial

Lake and Jefferson Memorial

Photo Gallery (continued)

Lincoln Memorial

Red Schoolhouse

Tank Farm

USS Arizona Monument

Vizcaya Museum — Miami

Flowers

Aster

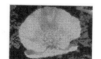
California Poppy

Coneflower

Fuchsia Closeup

Iris China Dragon

Poppy Red

Red Japanese Bridge

Terrestrial Orchid

Tulips Yellow Red

Waterlilies

Food

Avocado

Candy Corn

Carrots

Green Apples

Green Peppers

Jellybeans

Kisses

Kiwi

Kiwi and Strawberries

Lemons

Nuts

Pears

Pumpkin

Red and Yellow Peppers

Red Apples

Photo Gallery (continued)

Red Bell Pepper   Red Pears   Red Tomatoes   Sandwich   Yellow Bell Peppers

Landscapes and Scenery

Deception Pass in Fog   Desert Clouds   Ocean Beach   Rocky Shore   Salt Columns

Stop Sign in Desert   Wheat Field

Objects

Barrel Ends   Bottles and Clock   Christmas Tree Ball   Crossword Puzzle   Drafting Table

Flags   Honeycomb   I Love You in Sand   New   Old Stone Carving

Spiral   US Flag

Photo Gallery (continued)

People

Boy

Cheerleaders

Class Walk

Clown Face

Easter Bunny

Feeding the Birds

Fireman

Friends

Lineman

Marching Band

Playhouse

President Carter

President Clinton

Two Babies

Woman with Leaves

Sea Life

Anemone Fish

Angel Fish

Eel

Fish Factory

Fishing Net

Life Ring

Lobster

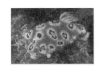

Nudibranch

Parrot Fish

School of Fish

Space

Astronaut for Sale

Astronaut on Moon

Astronaut Using Arm

Earth from Moon

Earth Skyline

Photo Gallery (continued)

Earth View

Jupiter and Moons

Launch Shuttle

Moon

Shuttle in Fog

Sports and Fun

Baseball

Equestrian Event

Equestrian Rider

Ferris Wheel

Lawn Chairs on Beach

Parachute Demo Team

River Rafters

Rock Climbers

Sail on the Beach

Water Skier

Transportation

The transportation photos are broken up into three categories (air, ground, and water), so go ahead and choose your preferred mode of travel:

Transportation by Air

737

B17

Concorde

Crop Duster

F117

F16

Goodyear Blimp

Hellcat Blue

Hot Air Balloon in Flight

P51

Photo Gallery (continued)

Seaplane
Landing

Side of Balloon

Thunderbird
Tails

Thunderbirds

Transportation by Ground

Aid Car

Black Street Rod

Caboose

Fire Engine

Fire Truck and
Ladder

Harley

Harvesting Corn

Horse Carriage

Industrial Truck

Old Horse and
Buggy

Red Car

Red Ford Street
Rod

School Busses

Steam Train

Street Rod on
Beach

Train

Transportation by Water

Aircraft
Carrier

Fishing Fleet at
Dock

Pirate Ship

Ship Yard

Trident
Submarine

Photo Gallery (continued)

Yacht

ClipArt

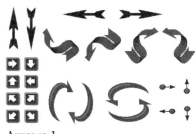

Arrows 1   Arrows 2

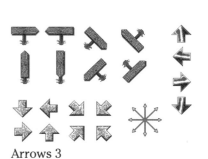

Arrows 3

Use for buttons or icons.

Buttons and Cursors

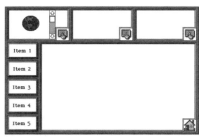

Buttons and Windows   Clouds

Clip Art (continued)

Curtain 1

Curtain 9

Earth 1

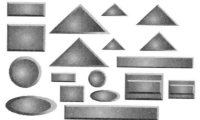
Gray Bev Buttons

HS in Blue

HS Screen

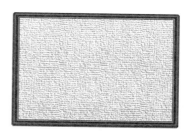
HS Textbox

Lit Stucco

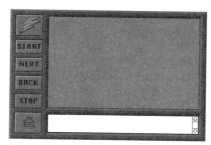
Presentation Screen

Clip Art *(continued)*

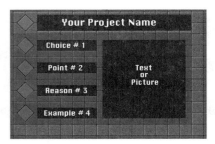

Presentation Screen 2

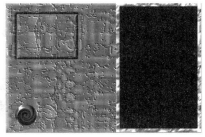

Rocky Interface

Space View

Stop Watch Art

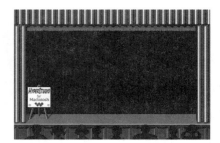

Theater 1

Theater 9

Dinosaurs

Acrocanthosaurus

Allosaurus

Archaeopteryx

Dinosaurs (continued)

Dilophosaurus

Gallimimus

Oviraptor

Plesiosaurus

Tyrannosaurus Rex

Velociraptor

Chasmosaurus

Anatosaurus

Hypsilophodon

Brachiosaurus

Iguanodon

Brontosaurus

Lambeosaurus

Maiasaura

Cliffs & Trees

Dinosaurs (continued)

Mammoth

Stegosaurus

Triceratops

Swamp Trees

Swamp Grounds & Plants

Dinosaur Parts 1

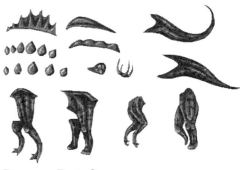

Dinosaur Parts 2

Multipædia

Artifacts 2

Artifacts

Multipædia (continued)

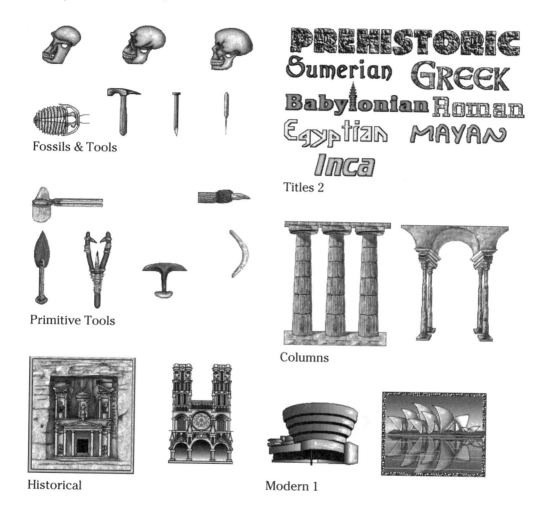

Fossils & Tools

Titles 2

Primitive Tools

Columns

Historical

Modern 1

Ruins 2

Ruins

Multipædia (continued)

Ruins 3

Taj Mahal

Taj Mahal 2

Clouds

Electricity & Magnetism

Electron Microscope

Heat

Light

Multipædia (continued)

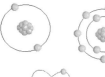

Molecules

Nuclear Energy

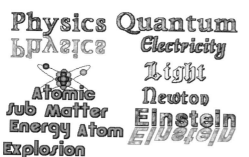

Titles

Books

Food

Mortar Board

Pennant Construction Kit

Sports

Multipædia (continued)

Medical Symbol Background

Ambulance

Ambulance

Medical Symbols

Medical Tools

Medical Tools 2

Medical Tools 3

Book Background

Chalkboard

Datatype 1

Multipædia (continued)

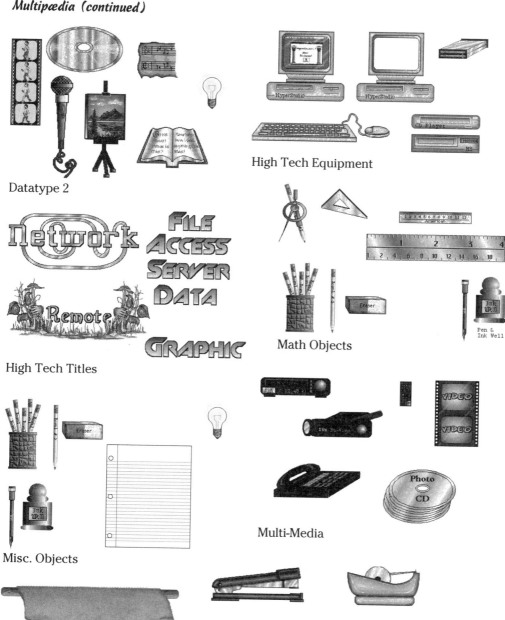

Datatype 2

High Tech Equipment

High Tech Titles

Math Objects

Misc. Objects

Multi-Media

Scroll

Supplies

Multipædia (continued)

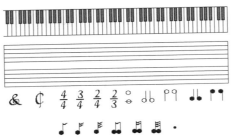

Music Construction Set

Palette & Brushes

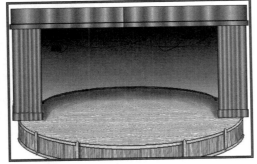

Stage

Stringed Instruments

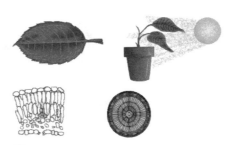

Plants

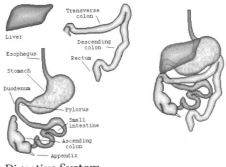

Digestive System

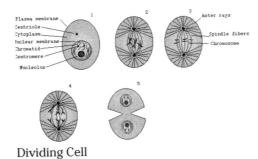

Dividing Cell

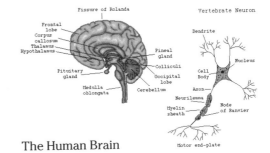

The Human Brain

Multipædia (continued)

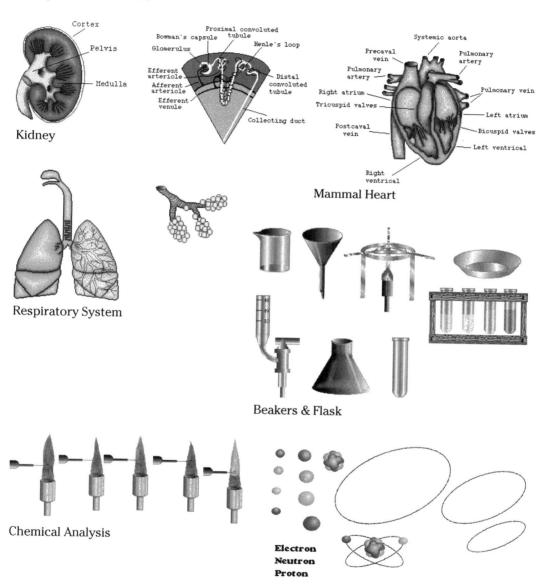

Kidney

Mammal Heart

Respiratory System

Beakers & Flask

Chemical Analysis

Electron
Neutron
Proton
Molecule
Molecule Construction Set

Multipædia (continued)

Periodic Table 640×480

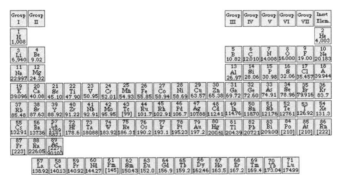

Periodic Table of Elements

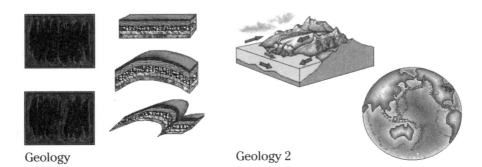

Geology   Geology 2

Multipædia (continued)

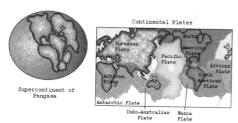

The Continents

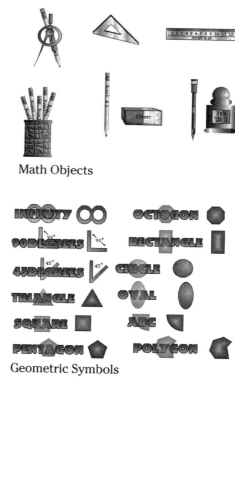

Math Objects

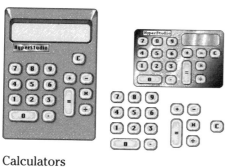

Calculators

Geometric Symbols

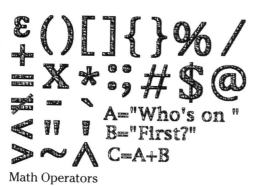

Math Operators

KidPix Studio

This program is also full of fun images and sounds.

Stamps

Each of the stamp sets shown here is available in the *KidPix, Moopies,* and *Stampimator* areas of *KidPix Studio.*

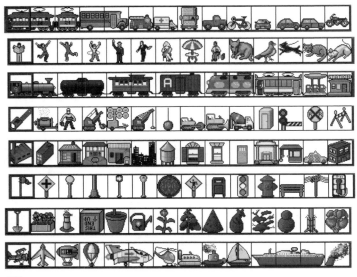

City

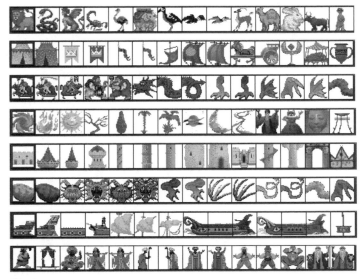

Genies

Stamps (continued)

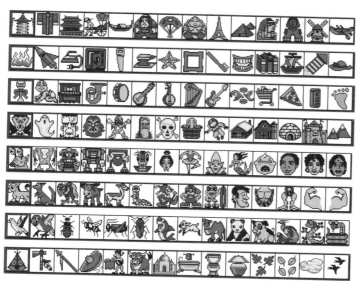

Hodgepodge

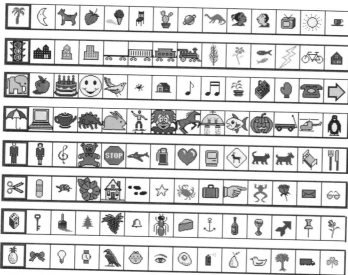

Original Stamps

Stamps (continued)

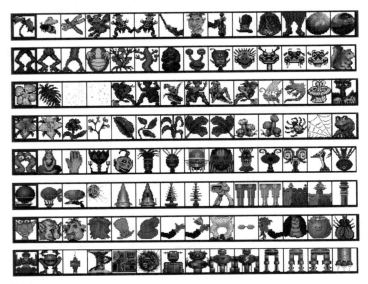

Pixies

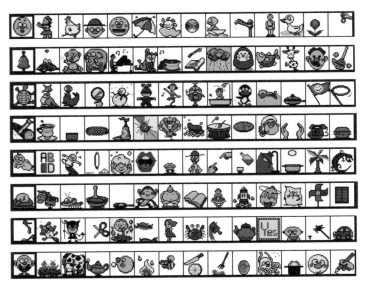

Teeny Toons

Stamps (continued)

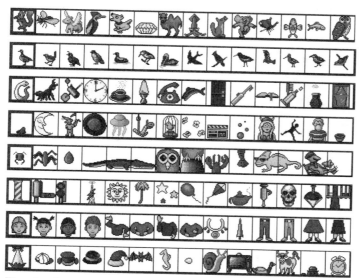

Toonies 1

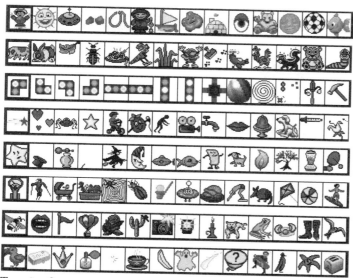

Toonies 2

Digital Puppets

Albert

Alien

Buster

Dragon

Dufus

Garden Sal

Nile Princess

Peteroo

Rasta

Shelly

Backgrounds

7 Daughters

Alaska Mountains

A Good Student

Amelia

Art Smile

At Play

Backgrounds (continued)

At Sea

At the Ball

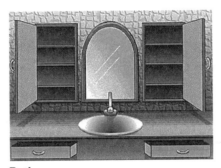

Bathroom

Beep Beep

Ben Excited

Big River

Backgrounds (continued)

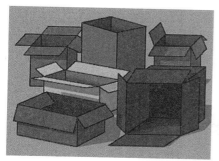

Boxes of Fun

Bridge

Bumpy Squash

Car Mirror

Carol, Me, and Cake

Castle

Backgrounds (continued)

Christmas Eve

Close Up

Coot

Crabs

Elephants

Fountains

Backgrounds (continued)

Garden Growing

Goose

Graveyard

Grouse

Gurgling Stream

Hands

Backgrounds (continued)

Hawk

Hibiscus

Kitten

Lake

Laundry

Leaves

Backgrounds (continued)

Llama

Log Home

Loon

Merganser

My Fort

Nice Dog

Backgrounds (continued)

Ocean Waves

Old Farm

Old Shed

On Stage

Open Road

Outer Space

Backgrounds (continued)

Owl

Palace

Path with Trees

Petrel

Pier

Pigeons

Backgrounds (continued)

Pisa

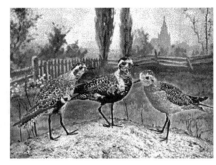

Plover

Polaroid Avocado

Pumpkin

Rainbow

Red Barn

Backgrounds (continued)

Rhinos

Riverbank

Rocks with Lizards

Ruins

Scottish Castle

Seagulls

Backgrounds (continued)

SF Palm

Small Town

Stroll

Sunset

Swans

Tea Time

Backgrounds (continued)

Technoscape

Throne

Train Station

Trees

Tunnel

Undersea

Backgrounds (continued)

Valley Lake

Venice

Vultures

Woman and Pig

Woodcock

Zebras

Appendix C
Mac Multimedia For Teachers CD

• •

*T*his CD is filled with demo versions of many of the programs listed within this book. And the coolest part of all is that the entire demo was put together using *HyperStudio*. That's right; the program that I'm recommending for you to use with your students created this professional CD. I love sharing information like that with my students — it helps to make their learning experience relevant. So share this CD with your students and let them have some fun, too!

Read Me First!

To enjoy this CD best, your Macintosh or compatible should have the following:

- ✔ a least a 68030, 68040, or PowerPC processor

- ✔ a double-speed CD-ROM drive

- ✔ at least 5 MB of free RAM (more, if you are using a Power Macintosh) to run most of the demos from the CD demo viewer interface

- ✔ a color monitor capable of displaying at least 256 colors

- ✔ a certain amount of free space on your hard disk drive *if you wish to copy or install some of the demos from the CD:* 10-50 megabytes or more

- ✔ the system software extensions necessary for your specific Macintosh to play QuickTime movies and sound found in the demo

For information about installing and using QuickTime, please see your computer manual, the *Mac Multimedia For Teachers* book, or other books published by IDG Books Worldwide, Inc. (Suggested titles include *Macs For Teachers* by Michelle Robinette; *Macs For Dummies,* 3rd Edition, by David Pogue; and *MacWorld Mac & Power Mac Secrets,* 2nd Edition, by David Pogue and Joseph Schorr.)

Important information on using the demos found on this CD-ROM

The demo viewer interface can run most — but not all — of the demos found on the CD-ROM. Some demos may behave differently from what the demo or your experience on a Mac may tell you.

You do *not* need to use the demo viewer to run all the demos. Each demo resides in a folder named after its manufacturer on the *Mac Multimedia For Teachers CD*. Just open the folder and then copy or install the demo to your hard disk. Or you can run the demo directly from the CD.

Note that some demos work properly only after you've changed some settings on your Macintosh or when you copy or install the demos directly to your hard disk.

Getting Started

1. Start by simply inserting the CD into your CD-ROM drive. Give it a few seconds, and you'll see the following icon appear on your desktop:

2. Double-click the CD icon; the following window will appear:

3. Double-click the Launch Me First! icon and you're set to go!

4. You'll see a few screens of information and finally come to the title screen. From this screen, click the prompt message that appears in the upper right-hand corner of the screen.

Click here to see the main menu.

5. Now you see the main menu screen. Clicking on one of the four chalkboards will take you to a more detailed list of products for you to preview.

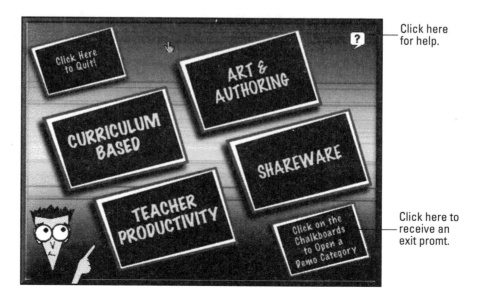

Click here for help.

Click here to receive an exit promt.

Go ahead and have some fun!

Note: All the software featured on the CD is available through any of the resources mentioned in Chapter 20.

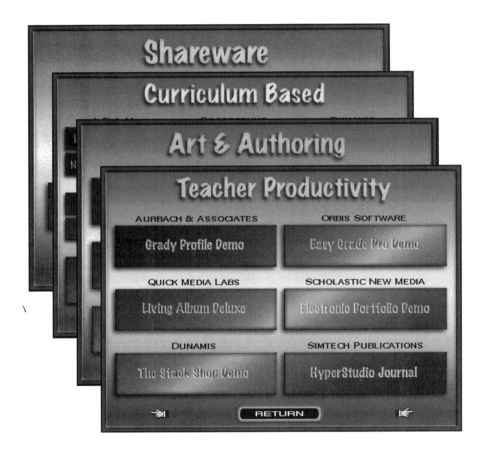

Summary List of Demos and Programs on the CD

Here's a quick alphabetical list of the demos and the programs included on the *Mac Multimedia For Teachers CD*.

Name	Company	Category
A.D.A.M.: The Inside Story	A.D.A.M.	Curriculum Based
Amazing Animation	Claris Corporation	Art & Authoring
Bailey's Book House	Edmark	Curriculum Based
ClarisWorks	Claris Corporation	Art & Authoring
Cruncher	Davidson & Associates	Art & Authoring
Easy Grade Pro	Orbis Software	Teacher Productivity
Electronic Portfolio	Scholastic New Media	Teacher Productivity
Flying Colors	Davidson & Associates	Art & Authoring
Grady Profile	Aurbach & Associates	Teacher Productivity
HyperStudio	Roger Wagner Publishing	Art & Authoring
HyperStudio Journal	Simtech Publications	Teacher Productivity
KidPix Studio	Brøderbund	Art & Authoring
Learn-to-Read	The Learning Company	Curriculum Based
Living Album Deluxe	Quick Media Labs	Teacher Productivity
Living Books	Brøderbund	Curriculum Based
Lost Mind of Dr. Brain	Sierra	Curriculum Based
Mark Twain	Poor Richard's	Shareware
Mega Sampler	Knowledge Adventure	Curriculum Based
Millie's Math House	Edmark	Curriculum Based
Morph	Gryphon Software	Art & Authoring
Multimedia Workshop	Davidson & Associates	Art & Authoring

(continued)

Name	Company	Category
Nine Month Miracle	A.D.A.M.	Curriculum Based
Our Times	Vicarious	Curriculum Based
Reading Journey	The Learning Company	Curriculum Based
Rudnick's Stacks	Dunamis	Curriculum Based
Stack Shop	Dunamis	Teacher Productivity
StuffIt Lite	Aladdin Systems, Inc.	Shareware
U. S. Map	Poor Richard's	Shareware

Categorized List of Programs on the CD

Here are the same demos and programs listed by category.

Art & Authoring

Name	Company
Amazing Animation	Claris Corporation
ClarisWorks	Claris Corporation
Cruncher	Davidson & Associates
Flying Colors	Davidson & Associates
HyperStudio	Roger Wagner Publishing
KidPix Studio	Brøderbund
Morph	Gryphon Software
Multimedia Workshop	Davidson & Associates

Curriculum Based

Name	Company
A.D.A.M.: The Inside Story	A.D.A.M.
Bailey's Book House	Edmark
Learn-to-Read	The Learning Company
Living Books	Brøderbund
Lost Mind of Dr. Brain	Sierra

Mega Sampler	Knowledge Adventure
Millie's Math House	Edmark
Nine Month Miracle	A.D.A.M.
Our Times	Vicarious
Reading Journey	The Learning Company
Rudnick's Stacks	Dunamis

Shareware

Mark Twain	Poor Richard's
StuffIt Lite	Aladdin Systems, Inc.
U. S. Map	Poor Richard's

Teacher Productivity

Easy Grade Pro	Orbis Software
Electronic Portfolio	Scholastic New Media
Grady Profile	Aurbach & Associates
HyperStudio Journal	Simtech Publications
Living Album Deluxe	Quick Media Labs
Stack Shop	Dunamis

Special Requirements for Some Demos

Here is a troubleshooting list of certain demos that may need special attention. Some of these demos have a Read Me file that may contain information about installing and using the demo.

A.D.A.M.: The Inside Story

✔ You will not be able to use your mouse or access menus while the demo is running.

✔ If you use a pivoting page-layout monitor, pivot your screen so that the monitor displays the desktop in *landscape mode* (longest horizontal width); otherwise, the demo screen may not appear properly in the center of the screen.

✔ If the audio begins to stutter, close the demo, restart the Mac with virtual memory OFF, and then return to the demo.

✔ The demo will repeat itself indefinitely. To quit at any time, press ⌘-Q.

Nine Month Miracle

✔ If you use your mouse pointer to access your menu bar or to start other programs, the demo may stop or behave strangely. When you return to the demo window, the demo will skip to the next full movie in its program, even if there were other items for display in the section playing at the time that you accessed the menu bar.

✔ If you use a pivoting page-layout monitor, pivot your screen so that the monitor displays the desktop in *landscape mode* (longest horizontal width); otherwise, the demo screen may not appear properly in the center of the screen.

✔ If the audio begins to stutter, close the demo, restart the Mac with virtual memory *off*, and then return to the demo.

✔ The "Done" button that appears within the demo screen is part of the demo's image and does not function.

✔ The demo will repeat itself indefinitely. To quit at any time, press ⌘-Q.

Mega Sampler

✔ Before using these demos, make sure virtual memory is turned *off*.

✔ Some of the demos require QuickTime to operate.

✔ To use the *3-D Dinosaur Adventure,* move the mouse forward like a car to move the screen forward and open the gates. Watch the icon at the bottom right of the screen; it will change appearance to instruct you to move the mouse left or right. When you arrive at the globe, use the mouse to spin it left or right and to choose the site you wish to view.

✔ Many of the buttons or menu choices in the Dinosaur demo are disabled. Features that are available appear as thought balloons with boldfaced text.

✔ To quit Knowledge Adventure's *Mega Sampler* demo, click the "Adventure Line" ship at the bottom right of the screen or press ⌘-Q.

Our Times

✔ *It is best to install this demo to your hard disk before using.* Read the demo's Read Me file before using this demo. An installer is included in the Vicarious folder on the CD.

✔ This demo requires QuickTime to operate. Make sure that you are using the latest QuickTime and support software.

✔ Before using this demo, make sure that virtual memory is turned *off*.

✔ The demo includes data for the decade of the 1940s only.

✔ You will not be able to access your menus or other programs while running this demo. To quit the demo at any time, press ⌘-Q.

The Stack Shop, Rudnick's Stacks

✔ When you quit the "Counting Candles" stack, the CD demo viewer will also quit. Double-click the CD demo viewer icon to return.

✔ Press ⌘-Q to quit the stacks at any time.

The Lost Mind of Dr. Brain

✔ You can skip the introduction to this demo by clicking the mouse.

✔ To quit the demo game, click the "switch" located in the upper-right portion of the screen, or press ⌘-Q.

Learn-to-Read, Reading Journey

✔ Be sure that virtual memory is *off* before running this demo.

✔ If you run this demo from within the CD demo viewer, the demo will tell you that you will be returned to the desktop to open the *Reading Journey* demo, when in fact, you will be returned to the CD demo viewer. To start the *Reading Journey* demo, click the button in the CD demo viewer.

KidPix Studio

✔ When you quit this demo, you will return to the CD demo viewer, but the viewer's windows may not be redrawn properly. As a result, the screen will be hard to read. If you click the left- or right-hand buttons, the screen will be redrawn properly.

ClarisWorks, Amazing Animation

- Copy the *ClarisWorks* software to your hard disk to get the best use of it.
- If you run *ClarisWorks* from within the CD demo viewer, *ClarisWorks* will quit the demo viewer.
- Read the Claris Read Me file, "Begin Here," for more information.

HyperStudio, Morph

- These demos will shut down the CD demo viewer in order to run.
- *Morph's* exporting functions are disabled.
- Files created in *HyperStudio Preview* are limited to one save. You can't save additional changes to a file if it has been closed.

Cruncher, Grady Profile, Easy Grade Pro

- *It is best to install these demos to your hard disk.* If you run it from the CD, the program may have problems remembering your preferences because it cannot save to the CD.

Living Album Deluxe

- *It is best to install this demo to your hard disk.* If you attempt to run it from the CD, the software may have problems opening the photo files needed for the program.
- This is a *beta* (a beta is software that is being tested and may not yet be completely perfected); it is possible that some features may behave somewhat inconsistently.

Electronic Portfolio

- Be sure that virtual memory is turned *off* before using this demo.

StuffIt Lite

- This is not a demo. When you click its button from the CD demo viewer, the installer will activate and attempt to install *StuffIt Lite 3.5,* a popular file compression for the Macintosh. If you do not want to install this software, click the installer's quit button.

Index

(continued)

(continued)

(continued)

(continued)

It's Just Simple Arithmetic

 **+**  **=**

HyperStudio   HyperStudio Journal

HyperStudio may be the easiest multimedia software you'll ever use in (or out of) the classroom but without a reliable resource you will probably never know the depth of this amazing program. Make HyperStudio Journal your resource and we'll show you how to make HyperStudio fly.

Each bimonthly issue of HSJ comes to you on disk and contains over 2.5 megs of the best HyperStudio stacks, New Button Actions (NBAs), clip art, sounds, HyperLogo scripts, useful freeware and shareware utilities, news and answers to your questions. There is no finer resource available... anywhere.

Visit us on the World Wide Web (http://www.tiac.net/users/simtech/HSJ.html) and see what HyperStudio users are so excited about.

HyperStudio Journal

Simtech Publications   Phone: 203/567-1173
134 East Street   Email: HSJournal@aol.com
Litchfield, CT 06759

Sign me up! I want the next 6 issues of HSJ for just $36.00

Name _____

Address _____

City/State/Zip _____

Email _____

☐ Bill me   ☐ Check enclosed   Charge my... ☐ VISA   ☐ MasterCard   ☐ American Express

☐☐☐☐ - ☐☐☐☐ - ☐☐☐☐ - ☐☐☐☐   ☐☐ / ☐☐

Account Number   Expiration Date

_____   _____

Cardholder Signature   Cardholder Name (please print)

The Multimedia Workshop CD

FREE ISSUE

Introducing **FamilyPC** — the fun, new computer magazine for teachers, parents and kids! **FamilyPC** is filled with creative ways to use technology at home and in the classroom. Your annual subscription also includes the Spring & Fall Educator Supplement — **SchoolPC**. And now you can try **FamilyPC** FREE — just clip out the coupon below and return to the address in the arrow or call toll-free **1-800-333-8783**. Refer to special FamilyPC code C498AAA.

FREE TEACHER HOME TRIAL

Published jointly by Disney (the world's leading expert on fun) and Ziff-Davis (the world's leading publisher of computer magazines), **FamilyPC** is dedicated to maximizing the computer advantage. Every issue includes:

- *Ratings & Reviews*
- *Creative Projects*
- *Deals & Discounts*
- *Mini-magazine just for kids*

MAIL COUPON TO:
FamilyPC
P.O. Box 400453
Des Moines, IA 50350-0453

☑ To receive your FREE trial issue of **FamilyPC**, just mail this coupon or call **1-800-333-8783**. If you like **FamilyPC**, you'll receive 9 more issues (for a total of 10) for the special introductory rate of $12.95. If **FamilyPC** is not for you, simply return the bill marked "Cancel." The free issue is yours to keep or give to a friend.

NAME

ADDRESS

CITY

STATE   ZIP

Canadian and foreign orders, enclose U.S. funds and add $10 for GST and postage. FamilyPC's annual newsstand price is $29.50. ©1995 FamilyPC

CE491AAA

IDG BOOKS WORLDWIDE LICENSE AGREEMENT

4. Limited Warranty. IDG Warrants that the Software and disc are free from defects in materials and workmanship for a period of sixty (60) days from the date of purchase of this Book. If IDG receives notification within the warranty period of defects in material or workmanship, IDG will replace the defective disc. IDG's entire liability and your exclusive remedy shall be limited to replacement of the Software, which is returned to IDG with a copy of your receipt. This Limited Warranty is void if failure of the Software has resulted from accident, abuse, or misapplication. Any replacement Software will be warranted for the remainder of the original warranty period or thirty (30) days, whichever is longer.

5. No Other Warranties. To the maximum extent permitted by applicable law, IDG and the author disclaim all other warranties, express or implied, including but not limited to implied warranties of merchantability and fitness for a particular purpose, with respect to the Software, the programs, the source code contained therein and/or the techniques described in this Book. This limited warranty gives you specific legal rights. You may have others which vary from state/jurisdiction to state/jurisdiction.

6. No Liability For Consequential Damages. To the extent permitted by applicable law, in no event shall IDG or the author be liable for any damages whatsoever (including without limitation, damages for loss of business profits, business interruption, loss of business information, or any other pecuniary loss) arising out of the use of or inability to use the Book or the Software, even if IDG has been advised of the possibility of such damages. Because some states/jurisdictions do not allow the exclusion or limitation of liability for consequential or incidental damages, the above limitation may not apply to you.

7. U.S.Government Restricted Rights. Use, duplication, or disclosure of the Software by the U.S. Government is subject to restrictions stated in paragraph (c) (1) (ii) of the Rights in Technical Data and Computer Software clause of DFARS 252.227-7013, and in subparagraphs (a) through (d) of the Commercial Computer—Restricted Rights clause at FAR 52.227-19, and in similar clauses in the NASA FAR supplement, when applicable.

Read Me First!

To enjoy this CD best, your Macintosh or compatible should have the following:

- ✔ a least a 68030, 68040, or PowerPC processor
- ✔ a double-speed CD-ROM drive
- ✔ at least 5 MB of free RAM (more, if you are using a Power Macintosh) to run most of the demos from the CD demo viewer interface
- ✔ a color monitor capable of displaying at least 256 colors
- ✔ a certain amount of free space on your hard disk drive *if you wish to copy or install some of the demos from the CD:* 10-50 megabytes or more
- ✔ the system software extensions necessary for your specific Macintosh to play QuickTime movies and sound found in the demo

For information about installing and using QuickTime, please see your computer manual, the *Mac Multimedia For Teachers* book, or other books published by IDG Books Worldwide, Inc. (Suggested titles include *Macs For Teachers* by Michelle Robinette; *Macs For Dummies,* 3rd Edition, by David Pogue; and *MacWorld Mac & Power Mac Secrets,* 2nd Edition, by David Pogue and Joseph Schorr.)

Important information on using the demos found on this CD-ROM

The demo viewer interface can run most — but not all — of the demos found on the CD-ROM. Some demos may behave differently from what the demo or your experience on a Mac may tell you.

You do *not* need to use the demo viewer to run all the demos. Each demo resides in a folder named after its manufacturer on the *Mac Multimedia For Teachers CD*. Just open the folder and then copy or install the demo to your hard disk. Or you can run the demo directly from the CD.

Note that some demos work properly only after you've changed some settings on your Macintosh or when you copy or install the demos directly to your hard disk.

Note: See Appendix C for more information.

IDG BOOKS WORLDWIDE REGISTRATION CARD

RETURN THIS REGISTRATION CARD FOR FREE CATALOG

Title of this book: Mac Multimedia For Teachers

My overall rating of this book: ❑ Very good [1] ❑ Good [2] ❑ Satisfactory [3] ❑ Fair [4] ❑ Poor [5]

How I first heard about this book:

❑ Found in bookstore; name: [6] _____

❑ Advertisement: [8]

❑ Word of mouth; heard about book from friend, co-worker, etc.: [10]

❑ Book review: [7]

❑ Catalog: [9]

❑ Other: [11]

What I liked most about this book:

_____

_____

What I would change, add, delete, etc., in future editions of this book:

_____

_____

Other comments:

_____

Number of computer books I purchase in a year: ❑ 1 [12] ❑ 2-5 [13] ❑ 6-10 [14] ❑ More than 10 [15]

I would characterize my computer skills as: ❑ Beginner [16] ❑ Intermediate [17] ❑ Advanced [18] ❑ Professional [19]

I use ❑ DOS [20] ❑ Windows [21] ❑ OS/2 [22] ❑ Unix [23] ❑ Macintosh [24] ❑ Other: [25] _____
(please specify)

I would be interested in new books on the following subjects:
(please check all that apply, and use the spaces provided to identify specific software)

❑ Word processing: [26] _____

❑ Data bases: [28] _____

❑ File Utilities: [30] _____

❑ Networking: [32] _____

❑ Other: [34] _____

❑ Spreadsheets: [27] _____

❑ Desktop publishing: [29] _____

❑ Money management: [31] _____

❑ Programming languages: [33] _____

I use a PC at (please check all that apply): ❑ home [35] ❑ work [36] ❑ school [37] ❑ other: [38] _____

The disks I prefer to use are ❑ 5.25 [39] ❑ 3.5 [40] ❑ other: [41] _____

I have a CD ROM: ❑ yes [42] ❑ no [43]

I plan to buy or upgrade computer hardware this year: ❑ yes [44] ❑ no [45]

I plan to buy or upgrade computer software this year: ❑ yes [46] ❑ no [47]

Name: _____ Business title: [48] _____ Type of Business: [49] _____

Address (❑ home [50] ❑ work [51] /Company name: _____)

Street/Suite# _____

City [52] /State [53] /Zipcode [54]: _____ Country [55] _____

❑ **I liked this book!** You may quote me by name in future
IDG Books Worldwide promotional materials.

My daytime phone number is _____

IDG BOOKS

THE WORLD OF COMPUTER KNOWLEDGE

❏ **YES!**

Please keep me informed about IDG's World of Computer Knowledge.
Send me the latest IDG Books catalog.